Dayt's face was shadowed, unreadable.

He lounged in the door frame without saying a word. Gypsy, nervous, said, "Well, I don't want to keep a hard-working farmer out any later than necessary, so I won't offer to make coffee."

She half hoped he'd say, "Go ahead, make it," but he didn't. In her three-inch heels, she found herself looking directly into the strong column of his neck, wondering how many women had clung there, kissing him. She cleared her throat and said briskly, "Well, good night, Dayton."

A low, soft chuckle was his reply. He loomed over her, warm, dangerously tempting, and all the more desirable because he made no attempt to embrace her. His hand reached to cup her chin, and he gazed long into her unflinching violet eyes. She blushed as the memory of his hard, seeking kiss came back with devastating force. I don't want him to kiss me! she panicked. I don't want to be hurt again!

Heartstorm

CAROL BLAKE GERROND

erenade/Serenata
BOOKS
of the Zondervan Publishing House
Grand Rapids, Michigan

A Note from the Author:
I love to hear from my readers! You may correspond with me by writing:
Carol Blake Gerrond
Author Relations
1415 Lake Drive, S.E.
Grand Rapids, MI 49506

HEARTSTORM
Copyright © 1986 by Carol Blake Gerrond

Serenade/Serenata is an imprint of Zondervan Publishing House,
1415 Lake Drive, S.E., Grand Rapids, MI 49506.

ISBN 0-310-47601-1

Edited by Lori Walburg
Designed by Kim Koning

Printed in the United States of America

86 87 88 89 90 91 / ZO / 9 8 7 6 5 4 3 2 1

To my father, the late Dean Blake, and my husband, Wayne Gerrond. You said I could do it!

chapter
1

AND SO SHE WAS HOME AGAIN. Gypsy Connor paused at
the base of three broad wooden steps, momentarily halted
by opposite emotions. She was deeply happy to be once
more at the northcentral Illinois farmhouse where she'd
sheltered in the downy warmth of family for nineteen of
her twenty-four years. But the reason for being here—
Gramps in the hospital near death—wrenched her with the
worst pain she'd ever endured.

Gramps couldn't go—not when she'd lost Grandma
years ago, not when her parents were again far away
answering a deeply felt missionary call. God couldn't do
that to her.

Gypsy firmed her shoulders under her plum raincoat and
pounced up to the rambling screened porch. Just as she
reached for the screen door handle, the whole stair railing
came off in her hand.

She stared stupidly at the decapitated rail posts, those
numb witnesses to age and neglect, and wondered if the
strength of her slender, healthy body had suddenly become
Amazonian. Then a rueful laugh broke her silence. She was
home, all right; the old house was just as cheerfully falling
apart as it had always been!

Gypsy crossed the wide porch, leaving the amputated handrail on a convenient shelf, and let herself into the house. The stale cold of the closed-up dwelling contrasted with the late April freshness of the outdoors; she shivered as she moved to the center of the long dining room and looked around.

Everything was just as it had been the day she'd left five years before: the big oak table and its sturdy chairs, her old piano in a corner, the white-painted brick fireplace massive along one wall, on its mantel the wedding portrait of her parents, beautiful almost-strangers to their only child.

She pivoted. Through the wide opening into the living room she saw the familiar mix of genuine antiques and twentieth-century overstuffed furniture that mingled unconstrained by any rules of decor. And over everything a layer of dust. That, too, was in character.

If only Gramps were here. Gypsy swallowed hard against a rush of longing. To be warm, to be safe once again in Gramps's protective love—

She heard footsteps coming up the stairs and across the porch, but she didn't turn, thinking she knew whose they were. "Jody?" she called abstractedly.

"Hello, Gypsy."

She whirled, startled, her heart lurching at the husky voice. The doorway to the porch framed a long, lean figure resting easily against the jamb, one masculinely sinewed hand on the doorknob.

"Dayt! You . . . surprised me!" Gypsy stammered. It wasn't just surprise that flushed her cheeks. There was also that incident of five years past accelerating the blood through her veins.

The man, big, blond, and good-looking in typical midwestern country attire of jeans, boots, and all-weather jacket, stepped fully into the room.

"Sorry, Gypsy, I didn't mean to scare you. I thought you heard me coming up the steps, but . . . I guess you were expecting someone else?" The straight sandy brows over Dayton O'Rourke's searching eyes lifted a bit on the question.

Oh, those eyes—they were a dark blue-green, the very color of the ocean, she knew, now that she'd seen an ocean, and shades of light played in them just as they did in great seas. And, like the ocean, they were dangerous.

Gypsy broke contact with them and brushed back a strand of the soft, dark hair that lay like a fluffy cloud about her head.

"Well . . . yes, I was. We just got here, after a side trip to the hospital, and I guess Jody must be stretching his legs, looking around the farm buildings. You knew about Gramps, didn't you?" She stuck her hands into her coat pockets to hide their nervous clenching. Just talking about Gramps, just the thought of his lying so still, so deathly wan in that hospital bed, set her trembling.

If Dayt felt much curiosity as to her traveling companion, he bypassed it to ask sympathetically, "How is your grandfather? I talked to your Uncle Worth yesterday, right after I heard about Jesse. He said the heart attack was massive."

Gypsy shuddered. "It was. Uncle Worth and Aunt May were at the hospital today when I got there. They said the doctors give him a fifty-fifty chance. He's in the coronary care unit, of course, so I . . . got to see him only long enough . . . to say hello. . . ." Her words choked off.

Dayton O'Rourke's athletic frame shifted again, and he ran a hand through his thick forelock, showing his uneasiness at the threat of her tears.

"He'll . . . he'll pull through, Gypsy. He's a tough old guy; you know that." His deep voice roughened in embarrassed compassion. "Oh . . . hey, I guess I'd better close the door, hadn't I?" he hurried on, obviously hoping to relieve a stressful moment. Just as he swung the door shut, he turned back to her, half jesting. "Or am I shutting out the man in your life . . . 'Jody' . . . wasn't it?" The glint in his eye was only partially bantering.

She was glad for the change of subject even if the new one irritated her. Of all the people she knew, Dayton O'Rourke was the last one to whom she owed any explanations about her personal life, especially after that night when he'd—

"Gypsy! What've we got to eat? I'm starved!" By the time the last word was uttered, a boy, thirteen, thin, and scraggly, burst like a noisy scarecrow into the house. Dayt stepped agilely aside to escape the wide-flung door. "Oh. . . hi," the youth tentatively greeted the tall stranger staring back at him. "Is that your car out there behind Gypsy's old clunker?"

At Dayt's eyebrow-cocked nod of affirmation, the boy whistled approvingly. "Wow! That's some ride! You buy a new 'Vette every year?"

"Jody!" Gypsy admonished, "you don't ask things like that!"

"Why not?" Jody turned back to Dayt, openly perplexed by Gypsy's scolding. "I mean, you must be doin' great to roll on that set of wheels!"

Dayt's slow-spreading grin and relaxed posture stopped Gypsy's further protest; after all, Jody didn't mean any harm. He simply didn't know any better. It was another point she'd have to go over with him when they were alone—one of the *many*.

"Well, yeah, you might say I do all right," Dayt agreed. "Tell me, Gypsy, who's your candid young friend?"

Gypsy stepped closer to Jody, who at five-five stood as tall as she, and looped her arm through his. "Dayton, I'd like you to meet my very special . . . boy, Jody Harris. I lived across from him and his mother in New York City, but now that she's . . . uh . . . gone, Jody lives with me. Jody, my part-time neighbor, Mr. Dayton O'Rourke."

Dayt took Jody's hand in a man-to-man shake as each acknowledged the introduction, then over the boy's head, his blue, piercing eyes threw a million questions at Gypsy's violet ones.

"How come you're a part-time neighbor?" Jody wanted to know. "You on the move all the time like Gypsy?"

"Not really," Dayt replied. "I'm a Chicago lawyer . . . I know, that's the worst kind. . . ." He forestalled Gypsy's possible putdown. "So I'm down here only on weekends and holidays. Mike Thompson is in charge of the actual farming of my place."

Remembering the steady stream of guests she'd seen pass through the gates of O'Rourke Farms in years gone by, and especially remembering the sleek, sophisticated female Chicagoans, Gypsy couldn't resist a gibe. "Mr. O'Rourke uses his country house mostly for recreational purposes, don't you, Dayt?"

Dayt's lips twisted in annoyed amusement, but he didn't bother to return her barb.

"He can afford to if he's a lawyer, Gypsy. They make really big—"

"The groceries are still in the car, Jody," Gypsy cut in brusquely. "If you'll bring them in, you can have some cookies to hold you over till suppertime. Not too many, though," she added.

"Okay, Gypsy. See you in a minute, Dayt . . . *Mr.* O'Rourke," Jody hastily amended at Gypsy's pointed throat clearing. He bounded outside to the car.

Gypsy hiked her shoulders and expelled a breath. "I never realized what strange creatures boys are until I got one of my own! I never know what he'll come up with next."

"What's his story, Gypsy?" Dayt's face was serious.

Gypsy moved to a window overlooking the porch and barnyard, not wanting Jody to slip back into hearing while she was divulging his background.

"When I moved in across from Jody and his mom . . . well . . . you can see how long it takes Jody to get acquainted! But I soon found out he needed all the bounce he could muster; Connie Harris was terminally ill."

"That's pretty rough," Dayt murmured.

"Connie didn't have the . . . best . . . kind of friends; I tried to do what I could for her. Toward the end her main worry was what would become of Jody."

"What about the boy's father? Why didn't he take him?"

"There is no father, that is, no legitimate one." Gypsy's eyes fastened on Dayt's. "There's no one for Jody except me. Before she died, about three months ago, Connie named me his legal guardian."

"Now wait a minute. She turned him over to you, a . . . a nearly total stranger?"

Gypsy recognized the logic in Dayt's skepticism. "Isn't that something? She knew I wasn't into drugs, alcohol, or wild sex. And Jody and I liked each other. With no real friend she could trust for just plain decency, she had to turn to a near-stranger."

Dayt let out a soft whistle. "Well." He studied her a second longer; she knew he was assessing her qualifications for the role as guardian. He laughed, not altogether humorously. "I never thought I'd see the virtuous Miss Mary Catherine Connor come home an unwed mother of a half-grown boy, yet!"

"You think it's funny?" The words snapped out of her before she could stop them; he'd touched a sore spot. "Just because I don't like being *mauled* by the local Casanova land baron, that doesn't make me some kind of prim and proper freak!"

"'Casanova land baron'?" he snorted, contemptuous. "My, aren't we fancy with our insults." His hands clamped onto his narrow hips in a gesture of irked impatience. "You haven't changed much, have you, Gypsy? Still got the fastest temper and the sharpest tongue in the West!" He chuckled, but it sounded more like a growl. "Good—!" He bit off an oath, took a half-step away, then turned on her. "Are you still sulking over that little bit of fun we had at my folks' thirty-fifth wedding anniversary party five *years* ago? Come off it, Gypsy. You didn't really mind it at all, at least not while it was happening."

The sardonic curl of his full lower lip struck her like fire to gunpowder. A crazy montage of strong arms, questing lips, kisses warm and demanding raised her anger to the boiling point. "That's *not* so!" she blurted. She opened her mouth, about to scald him with her wrath, but Jody was bounding up the steps, across the porch, into the room.

"Here's the groceries, Gypsy. Mind if I open the cookies?"

The brown paper bag in Jody's hand looked perilously inadequate in the face of his appetite, but it represented the buying power of her last five dollars. Heaven help them if Gramps didn't have some basic food supplies for them to fall back on until she could get a job.

"Sure, go ahead," she urged Jody as she and Dayt took less antagonistic stances. "Just put the sack out in the kitchen. And remember, not *too* many before supper."

Jody headed for the kitchen, and Gypsy forced herself to speak civilly to Dayt, mindful that Jody had been through enough in the past few months without being subjected to the animosity that rankled between her and the man who owned ten times the acreage of the small Connor farm.

"Well, it's . . . pretty cold in here, isn't it?" she managed to say. "I wonder if Gramps had the heat turned down, or if we're out of gas." When she checked the thermostat and saw that it was set at sixty-eight degrees, the awful truth was clear.

"I'll look at the gauge on the propane tank," Dayt offered. He exited, his footsteps on the stairs the fast, light tread of a natural athlete.

Gypsy hugged herself, less for warmth than to control the agitation he'd stirred in her. She began to pray, talking with God the way she did at any moment of her waking hours. *Please, Father,* she asked, *help me to hold my tongue. I can't go around flying off the handle at everyone who makes me mad—and he makes me mad! I've got to strengthen my patience. I've got to set a better example for Jody.*

She hadn't closed her eyes but had merely stared at the floor as she prayed. Hearing Dayt approach, she raised her eyes.

"It's empty."

Dayt's announcement was no surprise to her, but she said, reasonably enough, "Thanks for checking; I'll order more tomorrow." Inwardly, she cringed; unless Gramps had more cash on hand than he usually did, how could she pay for five hundred gallons of propane gas?

"I'll take care of it for you, Gypsy." Dayt's strong, clean-featured face revealed all too clearly his understanding of her situation. She felt all the worse to be thought a pauper.

"No, *I'll* see to it," she said firmly. Then she added swiftly, "But thank you, anyway."

Displeasure flickered across his face, but he, too, seemed resolved to behave well. Certainly it must be for Jody's sake; she knew all too well he could discard his inhibitions fast enough around *her*.

"Then I'll build a fire in the fireplace. I *do* have your permission to carry out that humble duty, haven't I?" he inquired, and this time the quirk at the corner of his mouth was almost friendly.

Gypsy's brow puckered, then straightened. Did she really want to keep up the sniping match? That seemed childish. She let a small grin form and spread to her eyes.

"Please, be my guest. With a little luck, you'll even find some chopped wood in the basement. Otherwise . . . " She gestured toward the door. "the backyard's full of trees."

"You're all heart, Gypsy!" Dayt playfully tweaked her nose between a calloused thumb and forefinger, then started through the basement door beside the fireplace.

"Oh, by the way," he said, popping back in, "if I can find some spikes, I'll fix the front handrail. What'd you do, tear it off to beat the kid with?"

Rats! Gypsy groused, chuckling, I wish he'd stay uniformly ornery. Then I'd know positively that I can't stand him!

She shrugged and started on the business of settling in. While Dayt got a brisk fire going, she and Jody carried in such luggage as they'd need before morning. She showed Jody into the spare bedroom, and she, of course, took her old room.

A thrust of nostalgia swelled her heart as she looked around the white-painted-furniture setting of her early years. Was it only five years ago?

Thwack! Thwack! That must be Dayt hammering the handrail into place. "Ouch . . . ah!" The smothered fulmination broke her pensive mood, provoking a snicker.

She moved swiftly into action, hanging clothes and making up a fresh bed. The physical exertion felt good after being cooped-up so long in her old Maverick. While she worked her eyes kept straying to the bulletin board over her bed; it was loaded with pictures and beloved memorabilia. A travel poster of "Exotic Rio"—how she'd dreamed of travel, adventures! Had it started with Gramps's summer-night tales of the gypsy caravans that, in his youth, had still roamed the countryside, sometimes tarrying in the Connor catalpa grove? She'd got her nickname from her endless requests for, "More gypsy stories, Gramps, please!"

Then there was a curled-edged snapshot of her sitting on the piano bench atop two Montgomery Ward catalogs, the first step to what was to become her career, "keyboard specialist." She paused, remembering the first time she, at four, had stood at the piano and suddenly picked out the tune of "Joy to the World!" If she'd launched into a Rachmaninoff concerto, Gram and Gramps couldn't have been more convinced of her genius!

From that moment on, if Gypsy wanted to play the piano, no chore, no duty interfered. There were music lessons for a while, but Gypsy had no patience for the stern demands of scales, fingerings, techniques. No, she wanted to play "by ear," and it was hard for her family to argue with her since almost anything she heard, she could reproduce.

True, the great classics were beyond her reach, but for many years they were also beyond her interest. Gospel, pop, country, soft rock, jazz—anything with alluring melody and catchy beat—that's what Gypsy preferred.

"I must have played for a thousand church services, weddings, funerals, school activities, parties," Gypsy murmured aloud, "before I ever thought of making money at it. And I don't regret a note of it; after all, God gave me the gift. Maybe that was his way of preparing me to play anything that had a keyboard—a real advantage in my job!"

The newest picture on the board was five years old; it was of Gypsy, slim and pretty with her fair skin and dark, natural curls, arms linked with her two fellow "slaves" at the local lumberyard office, taken just before she'd concluded, after two years of matching wits with typewriters and file cabinets, that she wasn't cut out to be an office worker.

And that's when Matt Morris saved my life, in more

ways than one, Gypsy reminisced. At a party, the infamous O'Rourke wedding anniversary, Matt Morris heard her playing and hired her on the spot to play the circuit of his Golden Lions, a chain of Old World-style restaurants stretching from the Midwest to the East Coast. The door opened to travel and adventure. And escape from that romantic renegade, Dayton O'Rourke, who'd—Gypsy swung her mind from what he'd done, vowing to put the whole episode out of her thoughts for good.

She emptied the last of her suitcase contents into a drawer and reflected that, true to her Connor roots, she'd come home with no more money than when she'd left; her job was interesting, but not lucrative.

She stepped to the window and pushed back the old lace curtains to look out at the farm's surroundings.

A century and a half ago when other New Englanders had flocked to the Midwest and carved rich farms from the Illinois wilderness, the Connors had settled on rolling, timbered land that wasn't as productive, but did possess a strange, wild grace. From that time on, they'd kept resolutely to their preference for that which enriched their spirits but left their pockets close to bare.

Gypsy's own parents had spent most of their adult lives as agricultural missionaries to such remote corners of the globe that it had seemed wise to leave her in the care of her grandparents. Right now mission authorities were trying to reach their post in New Guinea with word of Gramps's condition.

Gypsy'd heard the common saying, "The Connors are such good-hearted people. If they'd work as hard for themselves as they do for everyone else, they'd be rich!"

Well, there were worse things that might be said of a family, Gypsy counseled herself, as she exchanged her rumpled traveling suit for a pair of gray slacks and a warm red wool sweater. She brushed out her shoulder-length hair, feather-cut to frame the pixyish heart that was her face, then turned for one more glance at the bulletin board.

The thwacking had stopped. Gypsy sighed, touched with deepest tenderness the framed likenesses of Gram and Gramps at the center of her memory collection, and walked out of her bedroom. Dayt and Jody were sitting companionably before the good-smelling fire, Jody busily crunching down more cookies.

"Now, Jody," Gypsy reprimanded, "I told you to go easy on the cookies."

"Aw, Gypsy, there're only a couple left. I don't see any sense in savin' them because you don't eat 'em and Mr. O'Rourke has already had two or three."

"*No* more." Gypsy ended the controversy by snatching the nearly-empty bag from Jody's hand and setting it on the rough oak mantel. "Now, kiddo, you scoot into the bathroom and clean up. I'll have supper ready in a jiffy."

"Aw, shoot!" Jody grumbled as he got to his feet and shambled off toward the bathroom, muttering all the way.

"He . . . uh . . . he's never learned the meaning of the word no," Gypsy explained to Dayt. "His mom just kind of let him do as he pleased."

"He also hasn't learned the meaning of 'girls'," Dayt observed wryly. "When he does, he'll be living in the shower when he isn't working on his hair or worrying about his complexion."

Gypsy laughed. "I wouldn't know about that. At least

he's not street-wise; that's pretty remarkable. But he's spent a lot of time alone in an apartment; it'll take some doing to get him used to . . . normal . . . life."

Dayt's raised eyebrows wrinkled his broad forehead. "And *you're* going to give him a 'normal' life? Teach him discipline?"

"Why, yes." She stiffened at his incredulous tone. "I don't know why I can't as well as anybody."

"First of all, you're an entertainer; that's not conducive to a 'normal' lifestyle. Secondly, you yourself aren't exactly familiar with discipline."

"Me? Undisciplined? What are you talking about?"

"I did a lot of growing up in this neighborhood, remember, Gypsy? I saw how you had your grandparents wound around your little finger. You never had to do anything you didn't want to."

I will *not* blow up! I will *not* blow up! she schooled herself. In a voice calm, yet dangerously polite, she informed him, "I agree, Dayton, that an entertainer doesn't keep quite the same hours as say, you, a lawyer, but as to discipline, believe me, the last five years have taught me all about tailoring my likes to suit others."

That was an understatement. She loved making music; still, although her fingers usually took on a life of their own, conjuring rich beauty that pleasured as it flowed, there were times when her hands felt like wood, when they had to be forced into one perfunctory rendition after another. Wasn't that discipline?

Dayt gazed at her a long time, and once again she could almost hear the whir of his mental computer matching her abilities against her deficiencies and coming up short. "Well," he drawled finally, "we'll see, won't we?"

Why doesn't he go home? Gypsy gritted to herself. It's nearly six o'clock, I've got a hungry boy to feed, and Mr. Superior doesn't know enough to leave. Go home, unwanted one, she silently willed.

Jody came out of the bathroom, running a comb through the thick mop of rusty-red curls that tumbled about his head, and reported cheerfully, "There's no hot water, Gypsy, so I guess I won't have to take a bath tonight, huh?"

Would the unpleasantries of this hour never cease?

"Of course there's no hot water, Jody; we're out of gas for the heater. But you'll have your bath. We'll heat a bucket or two of water on the stove. *It's* electric, thank goodness." No Connor, Gypsy knew, ever went through a day without a bath. Their farming and housekeeping might be haphazard, but their personal cleanliness was absolute.

"You're welcome to come over and shower at my place tonight," Dayt offered. "It would save you a lot of trouble. In fact, if you want to spend the night—"

"Thanks, but no," Gypsy interrupted. "We'll be just fine."

Jody's face fell at her refusal of an effortless hot shower, but it brightened again almost at once. "Say, Mr. O'Rourke, why don't you stay and have supper with us? Gypsy cooks real good stuff."

Gypsy nearly sank through the floor; what was the matter with that kid? Didn't he realize that the hot dogs and packaged macaroni and cheese she'd bought for their meal was hardly the kind of dinner a man like Dayton O'Rourke was used to? But what could she say now? Another ingrained Connor rule was that no one left their homes at mealtime without a warm invitation to partake of whatever was available. They took seriously the Lord's injunction to share "even a cup of cold water."

"Yes, Dayton, wouldn't you like to stay?" she forced out. *Please* go home! her mind begged.

"Oh, I don't want to be any bother—"

"It's no bother, is it, Gypsy?" Jody pleaded. He turned to Dayt. "She can make almost anything taste good, even vegetables."

Her poor efforts in the kitchen meant that much to Jody? In an instant Gypsy's misgivings collapsed. Her heart smote her; she'd got so engrossed in her own problems she'd forgotten that Jody, who'd never had much of a home life anyway, was now completely dependent on a young woman he'd known only a few months for whatever stability and warmth she could scrape together. She wanted, more than anything else, to turn this somewhat dismal homecoming into something special, something good for him.

She put an arm around Jody's thin shoulder and smiled at Dayt. "If you've got a cast-iron stomach like Jody, you're more than welcome to stay." And I hope a fairy godmother comes along right away! she added mentally.

Out of the blue, a memory struck her: something that Grandma used to do on dull days when the young Gypsy was restless for a bit of novelty.

Dayt reciprocated her smile, albeit a trifle warily. "Well, if you really want me to—

"We do. And I've got a job for you two gents."

"Oh, oh, Jody, I was afraid of that!" Dayt grinned. "Women usually have something up their sleeve when they turn smiley. Okay, Gypsy, shoot—what do we have to do?"

Gypsy laughed outright. For the first time since she'd got the call about Gramps, she felt the sparkle that usually animated her personality. "I'd like you to go outside and cut three good hot-dog roasting sticks. We're going to have a picnic right here in front of the fireplace!"

The sheer sense of fun lighting Jody's eyes was all the incentive Gypsy needed to set aside her troubles and concentrate on fixing "the best stuff." She pushed up her sweater sleeves and started to work. While the macaroni cooked, she cleaned carrot and celery sticks, fanning the ends to make them more festive. Some extra cheddar from Gramps's stock enriched the macaroni and cheese. Dessert? There was only one respectable finale for a weenie roast, wasn't there? Marshmallows! She found an ancient bag hiding behind the breakfast cereal. Maybe toasting would tenderize them to reasonable edibility.

A cheery red tablecloth spread on the floor in front of the fireplace greeted Dayt and Jody when they returned bearing sharpened sticks, and they helped carry in the place settings and food. Then the three sat Indian-style, Jody facing the fireplace, Gypsy and Dayt each other.

Gypsy hesitated a moment, then, as was the Connor dinnertime custom, reached for the hands of the other two. "Dayton," she requested softly, "would you care to ask the Lord's blessing?"

Jody took her right hand and Dayt the left; his warm clasp transmitted a little shock of strength that flowed through her and on to the boy who joined them in a circle of three. As they bowed their heads for Dayt's simple,

"Bless, O Lord, this food to our use, and accept our thanks for Thy bounty," Gypsy felt unexpected pleasure seep over her. How good it was to share, even for a short time, the nourishment of Christian fellowship, the spiritual food that gave one the courage to carry on, the faith to let go of problems not immediately solvable and enjoy the good at hand.

After the blessing, Gypsy announced, bubbling with fun, "Messieurs, the *Chez Conneur* is now open for your dining delight." Her hand gestured grandly to the package of weiners. "May I suggest the broiled *Steak Tubulaire* with *Casserole de Macaronee?*"

The merriment was continuous during the impromptu picnic. Everything was funny, including the inevitable loss of one hot dog to the fire when Jody, cutting up, hooked his spitted "tube steak" on a snag. Since he'd already devoured four hot dogs and half the macaroni and cheese, Gypsy didn't worry that he'd go hungry.

A soft spring rain began to fall and the cozy patter on the roof and windows held them a long time before the fire. Dayt kept them in stitches with tales of his K.P. duties in navy boot camp, and Gypsy served up some of her choice stories of life behind the restaurant world scene.

"But the worst mess," she declared, "was the night in Hoboken when I was playing this super new electronic organ that could do just about everything but sing. I was into my best Stevie Wonder imitation when a waiter came past me with a loaded tray on his shoulder and—I swear it was *deja vu*—all of a sudden I *knew* what was going to happen, and it did; he tripped, went sprawling, and the whole trayful of food sailed right through the air to land on me and my keyboard! Can you imagine all that food trickling into the works of a mega-thousand dollar organ? And me sitting there with broiled fish on my head?"

Dayt's full-bodied laughter was a satisfying underscoring of Jody's whoops, and Gypsy herself giggled helplessly at a situation that hadn't seemed a bit funny when it happened.

"Oh," she gasped, wiping her eyes, "I've got to have one more gorgeous, gooey, toasted marshmallow to salve my dignity! Hand me one, will you, Dayt?"

"I'll do better than that; I'll toast it for you," he stated gallantly. In a few seconds the burnt delicacy was wafting before her nose, cooling off enough for her to demolish it. Just as she reached to take it off the stick, Dayt removed it and held it for her to eat from his fingers.

"Doing my Boy Scout good deed," he wisecracked to Jody, who immediately stuck two or three of the toughened blobs onto his own roasting stick.

Gypsy hesitated; somehow it seemed so intimate to accept food from a man's hand. A soft flush crept from the base of her neck up over her head. Oh, for heaven's sake, why did she have to think of it that way? It was nothing— nothing like that to Dayt, she was sure. She kept her eyelids down and opened her mouth; she felt his fingers brush her lips as they slid the soft morsel into her mouth; her jaws were paralyzed. Instead of chewing, she just sat there burning with an awareness that couldn't escape Dayt's notice. He'll think I'm the greenest novice in the country, getting so worked up over a mere marshmallow, she silently groaned.

Deliberately, Gypsy forced her eyes up to Dayt's; her color turned to flame as she met a gaze so knowing she was sure he saw her thoughts. Without a word he lifted a lazy forefinger to wipe a dot of clinging goo from the center of her lower lip. His eyes still holding hers, he dispatched the bit of marshmallow with the tip of his tongue. The amused taunt of his blue-green gaze sent an electric pulse zinging into her strangely vulnerable heart.

"Good," was all he volunteered, still mischief-eyed.

Gypsy came to life. She chomped down on the warm sweetness in her mouth and blurted, half-choked, "I . . . I think I'd better make us some coffee!" She scrambled to her feet, unable to stay so close to Dayton O'Rourke for even one second more.

chapter

2

THE FIRE GLIMMERED, satiated by its former ardor. Dayt and Gypsy sat propped against chair legs and sipped second cups of coffee, Jody banished to bed after a stove-heated bath and stern orders from Gypsy. Dayt's long, muscular legs stretched beside the tablecloth; he seemed absorbed in the low-hissing embers.

Through lash-shuttered eyes, Gypsy watched the play of firelight over the thick, well-shaped hair, the sharp handsomeness of a face both expressive and intelligent. Around his eyes and lips were fine crinkles that came from thirty some years of more smiles than snarls.

She had to give Dayt one point: he was comfortable with his good looks, not vain. Peacockery in a man was intolerable to her. But once she'd let her awareness of his outward charm override her judgment. That must never happen again. Still, it *was* hard to ignore his attractiveness. Change the subject, her brain ordered.

She sat forward, the all-polite hostess. "How are your parents, Dayt?" She liked the husband-wife lawyer team who, among other kindnesses, had from her childhood encouraged her to come play the big Steinway at O'Rourke Farms any time they were down from Chicago.

A grand piano! What a thrill it had been to arouse splendrous chords from its majestic depths!

"They're fine, Gypsy, down in Arizona. They've semiretired, turned almost everything over to me, you know. Mom says her arthritis behaves better in a hot, dry climate."

"You mean I won't be seeing them over at the farm any more?"

"Probably not, unless you stay a long time." Dayt shifted to poke at an ember with a roasting stick. "How long *are* you planning to stay, Gypsy?"

"Probably a long time."

He turned, eyeing her, surprised. "You are? What about your career? There aren't any Golden Lions around here."

Gypsy gazed into the smoldering fragments, trying to see a logical future. "I know. But aside from getting Gramps back on his feet, I've got Jody to think about. Underneath all his resilience—and he's got a lot of it—there's some confusion, some anger. He needs stability. So I think for a while, at least, we'd better stay put right here."

"Mmm." Dayt's murmur was contemplative. "If that's the case, then there're some things we've got to discuss, for instance, what you'll live on."

Gypsy's glance swung to his. What business was that of his?

He homed in on her thoughts. "Before you fire up, it's my business because your grandfather has given me power of attorney. His finances, his property—they're under my care."

"Wh–why?" Gypsy was dumbfounded. Why would Gramps turn his affairs over to an outsider? "Are you trying to say I can't live here?" she bristled.

Dayt slung down the roasting stick with an impatient sigh. "Will you get that chip off your shoulder? Just listen to a few facts before you go into another one of your melodramatic rages. Number one: your grandfather has been in poor health for some time—"

"Why didn't someone tell me? Why wasn't I called until he was nearly dead?" Gypsy's voice rang accusingly.

His voice steely hard, Dayt cut her off. "He didn't want you to know. As usual, his main concern was that you be free to live by your music—'bless the world with it'—that's how Jesse always put it," he added ironically.

Gypsy's eyes blazed angry fire. No one, but *no* one got under her skin like this rude, arrogant—"Apparently *you* don't consider it any blessing," she spluttered.

"I consider it good, truly entertaining, but not anywhere near what it could be if you'd had the grit to stick to your piano lessons, gone on to college or conservatory—"

"Oh, sure!" Gypsy leaped to her feet. "I had just *loads* of money for college or conservatory!" Once again her temper kicked over the traces and took charge of her mouth. "You seem to forget, Dayton O'Rourke, that the Connors aren't big-city rich like the O'Rourkes. *We* don't have a bunch of farms just because we need a tax write-off!"

His lunge to his feet caught her so by surprise she let out a little yelp, a breathless "Oh!"

"Don't you ever say that about my family!" he thundered at her. His face, dark with anger, loomed threateningly above hers, almost nose-to-nose. "My parents both worked hard for every cent they have, and they've poured a small fortune into the poor-grade, misused farmland they bought to bring it back to life. They've supported every worthwhile activity in this community. My dad offered to loan you interest-free money to continue your schooling, Gypsy, but no, you were too *proud* to accept his help. Or so you said. If you want my opinion, I think you were just too lazy to take him up on it!"

"Lazy?" The wearisome, desperate struggle of the past five years to grow from talented amateur to seasoned professional—she was *lazy*? "Where do you come off, calling me—"

"Gypsy! Is he bothering you?"

The embattled pair at the fireplace jerked apart to see Jody, pajama-clad and rumple-haired, poised in the double doorway to the living room with Gypsy's old baseball bat, relic of grade-school recess games, in hand.

"Jody!" Gypsy gasped. Was he going to attack Dayt?

Dayt stepped back and onto the macaroni bowl, sending it spinning across the room.

"Jody, it's all right! It's all right, honey!" Gypsy exclaimed. "Dayt and I were just having a . . . word fight."

"Are you sure?" Jody's boyish voice was high with strain. "You were getting pretty loud." His thin hands clutched the bat in white-knuckled readiness to use it.

Shame enveloped Gypsy. She had done it again—let her explosive temper spoil what had been a good evening for Jody and for all three of them. What had she gained? Was wrangling with Dayton O'Rourke really worth upsetting Jody, who had experienced God-knew-what as the son of sweet, weak Connie Harris?

"Jody," she soothed, pushing her voice down to normal, "don't worry about me. I guess I'm just an old crab tonight from all the tension we've been under lately. You go back to bed." She patted his arm, trying to find some way to reassure him that nothing really dreadful was about to happen. "I promise, if Dayt and I decide to put on boxing gloves and have a go at it, we'll call you to referee!"

Her little joke broke the tension, and Jody, visibly relieved, grinned tentatively at Dayt, then turned to go to his room. "Well, Okay. 'Night, Mr. O'Rourke," he mumbled.

Dayt watched him for a second, then walked over to put a hand on his bony shoulder. Jody pivoted, his grip involuntarily defensive on the ball bat as he faced the big man.

"Listen, Jody, I just want you to know you did the right thing to come out and make sure Gypsy was all right. I feel a lot better about her living here in the country now that I know she's got you to protect her."

Jody's grin made a slow return, but now it bore something new. Gypsy knew she'd just witnessed one of those definitive experiences that change a boy into a man. Dayt's approval had done more for Jody's self-esteem than any words Gypsy could add, and she was grateful that some bit of good had come from her blowup.

"Well . . . uh . . . good night, Mr. O'Rourke, Gypsy," Jody said with a note of new dignity in his voice.

"Dayt, call me Dayt," the tall blond man requested of the skinny teenager.

"Sure Dayt. I'll be seein' you, right?"

"Right." Dayt gave Jody's shoulder a manly cuff as the boy strode off toward his room. Gypsy could have sworn he looked an inch taller!

At the sound of Jody's door closing, Gypsy and Dayt turned back to each other.

31

"Well, can we have a sensible discussion now?" Dayt inquired calmly.

Gypsy took a deep breath, marshaling all her determination to behave sanely. "Yes, I think we can. But first, thank you Dayt, for what you said to Jody. He hasn't had many words of praise from adult males." She thought of some of the men Connie had gone out with. Definitely not the type to applaud a boy's defense of his guardian's welfare.

"I meant what I said, Gyps. He's an all-right kid. But now, let's get back to the matter at hand—how you're going to live. Is there a place with better light where I can show you some figures?"

"We can use Gramps's office," Gypsy said, glad to enter a dispassionate phase in their dealings. She led the way into the small room where Gramps kept his desk and farm records, as well as a dozen items that had no bearing whatsoever on his farming operation. She turned on lights and hastily cleared a pile of old magazines off the desk chair so Dayt could sit, then pulled up another chair herself.

Dayt took a case from his pocket and donned a pair of large-lensed, rimless glasses. Gypsy stared at him.

"When did you start wearing glasses, Dayt?" she inquired. He looked wonderful in them, sophisticated, capable.

"When the fine print started looking like mush," he replied. "For a lawyer, that's the time to put away vanity and put on the specs."

"Well, you look—awfully good in them."

"You look awfully good *through* them," he returned. "Now, let's forget the physical aspects of our relationship and get down to business," he continued dryly. "Your grandfather wanted me to take complete charge of his affairs, so I have." He wrote several swift, sharp figures on a scrap of paper.

"Dayt, I'm not trying to challenge you, but why are *you* in charge? Why not Uncle Worth, since he and Gramps own everything together?"

Dayt swiveled his chair toward Gypsy, settling back to peer at her through glasses that increased the impact of his blue-green eyes. He tapped his pencil against the corner of his mouth, where a semiquizzical smile teased. "Gypsy, honey," he said, the endearment slipping out as naturally as breath, "you have to ask that?" His gentle tone took any scorn out of the question.

"Well—" she faltered.

"I don't know a man with more intelligence or more integrity than your Uncle Worth, or your grandfather, for that matter. But when it comes to business. . . ." He paused, letting her mentally fill in the blank.

Gypsy knew as well as he that Gramps and Uncle Worth were woefully haphazard in financial affairs. She nodded her head in silent acquiescence.

"So," Dayt swiveled back to the desk, "here's a brief picture of how things stand. This is what Jesse has in his personal checking account." He pointed to what even Gypsy, unaccustomed as she was to affluence, could see was a pitifully slim balance. "And this," he indicated another figure, "is what he's got put away in a savings account to serve as part of your legacy when he's gone."

A few thousand dollars, that's all it was, but it brought tears brimming to Gypsy's eyes. She knew what it meant for a Connor to meet all his bills on time—which he usually did—let alone put away anything toward the future. Gramps must have sacrificed his own wants to save that money.

"I hope ... I hope I don't inherit that for years and years!" she whispered fervently. "Not if it means losing Gramps!"

"Of course, Gypsy. I know how you feel." Dayt did her the kindness of looking away while she dabbed her eyes dry.

"But the plain fact is, you may have to use that money long before your grandfather dies. Now, just let me explain," he insisted when she opened her mouth to protest. "Jesse and Worth pay all their farming expenses out of one account, then each has a separate fund for personal use. For the past few years, Jesse has turned nearly all his share of the income over to Worth to support that big family of his, and it still isn't enough. Did you know your uncle is teaching part-time to make ends meet? Biology at Sauk Valley High."

"Yes, I know. Aunt May wrote me."

"Then you see you're in a serious situation. Possibly you and Jesse could have managed, but now, with a growing boy to feed and clothe—" He didn't finish, nor did he need to.

"I know, Dayt," she replied, then looked him full in the eyes. "But there was no way at all I could walk off and leave that boy to go into an orphanage. I'm the closest thing to family he's got, and if I have to scrub floors to keep us together, then that's what I'll do."

Dayt's gaze was long and probing. She didn't flinch; she meant every word she'd said.

"I understand that, too," he said finally, "but you've got to realize Jody is going to consume massive quantities of food; he's going to outgrow clothes almost before you get them home from the store. I know something about teenage boys, Gyps, I've been one. They cost money without even trying."

Gypsy sat, blinking hard to hold back tears of weariness, worry, and frustration. It had been such a long day, with a twelve-hour drive during which she'd had plenty of time to evaluate her precarious financial position and the enormous burden she'd taken on by claiming Jody as her ward. Then the painful visit to the hospital to find her beloved Gramps too weak to do more than whisper her name before the nurse shooed her out of the room, and next the meeting with Aunt May and Uncle Worth, who, of course, assured her she and Jody would want for nothing they could provide. And her keen determination that by hook or by crook, she'd not be a parasite on their already overstressed pockets. She would make her own way, support herself and Jody, give him a good, solid home. But how? Right at the moment the question seemed crushing.

"Gypsy?" The word was soft, kind. She found her right hand sheltered in the hard warmth of Dayt's strong-fingered clasp. Why did kindness from him rattle her far worse than his arrogance? She bit her lip to stop its trembling and met his concerned gaze.

"I didn't want to lay all this on you tonight, but there are a few things we have to take care of right away. The gas, for instance. I'll call the propane dealer first thing tomorrow and get your fuel tank filled. Then I'll set up a charge account at Sauk Valley Market Basket so you can get all the groceries you need and just sign a tab—"

"But you just showed me Gramps's checking account. There's not enough there to cover all this—"

"Hold your horses, Gyps. There *will* be—"

"No!" She threw her head with the characteristic little snap that always accompanied her impatience. "It would be your money, wouldn't it? No Connor has ever accepted charity, and I won't be the first!" She pushed back her chair and stood, pulling her hand out of Dayt's.

His glasses came off in a slow swerve that boded ill for her defiance. His face took on flinty lines she'd never noticed there before. He stood, and she became intensely aware of the sheer physical power of the man. She stepped back, a little catch in her breath betraying her uncertainty.

"Mary Catherine, the time has come for you to grow up and accept the fact that you can't always have things the way you want them. Right now you've got a boy who looks a lot like a walking skeleton—for that matter, you're pretty skinny yourself—and you're not in any position to provide the two of you with three square meals a day and a roof over your head. If you want to stay in your grandfather's house, you'll do as I say, and I say I'll see to the paying of your bills."

There was dead silence. Gypsy, mindful that he who controls the purse strings controls a lot, fought back the white-hot rage that drove out her fatigue like a shot of adrenalin. That he had struck on truth was all the more maddening. She stood, seething, glaring into his chest, since that was the part of him level with her eyes.

Dayt tipped up her stubbornly-set face to his hard scrutiny. "Get one thing straight, Mary Catherine: you won't buffalo me the way you always have your grandfather." One finger brushed softly over the corner of her grim mouth. "But it may be fun thwarting your spoiled-baby antics while you try."

She pushed his finger aside and whipped away from him, purposefully striding to the front door, where she stood ramrod straight, hand on the doorknob in a none-too-polite reminder that he'd outstayed whatever welcome he'd ever had. "I'll see that you're paid back every penny, Dayton O'Rourke, just as soon as possible."

He ambled over to retrieve his jacket flung over a chair. Shrugging himself into it, he said, "Don't worry about it. When your grandfather is able to handle it, I'll work out something with him and Worth." He zipped the jacket unhurriedly, all the while surveying her with coolly superior eyes.

"Oh, really? I suppose you think this farm, this 'poor grade, misused land,' will eventually end up as part of your 'reclamation project,'" she sneered spitefully, "so why not now?"

As he deliberately strode toward her, she backed into the wall. "You're so right, Gypsy," he pronounced melodramatically, hovering only inches from her startled eyes. "Look at my mouth. See that mustache sprouting on my upper lip?"

The clean warmth of his breath fanned her tender lips, unnerving her more than she wanted to show.

"By the time I have handlebars worth twirling, I'll have this whole farm in my greedy possession. And you know what else?" He licked his lips lustily.

He's laughing at me again! she fumed, but she knew there was no escaping him until he'd acted out his little drama. "Please step back, Dayton," she ordered rather shakily, realizing the full effect he had over her even when he was playing the clown.

"Mwha! ha!ha!ha!" His hollow, bad-man chortle was soft near her ear and sent her heart pounding. "That's the other part of my plan, me fair beauty, haven't you guessed? After I kick your family off the old homestead, I'll keep *you* here as my woman."

She meant to flatten his ego with some blasting retort, but the pure silliness of his waggling brows and smirking grin caught her off guard. She bit her lips to stop their capricious surrender to laughter.

"You forget I'm just a spoiled brat," she challenged airily.

"Yeah!" His chuckle brought the blood racing to her heart. "You let me be the judge of that."

"*That* does it! Go home, Dayton O'Rourke, before I call out my protector," she demanded, pushing him back.

"Sure, Gypsy." He opened the door to the porch. "I'll see you tomorrow, after I send the kid out for pizza—to Chicago!"

His self-confident laugh drifted all the way across the porch, down the steps, and into his high-powered sports car. Gunning the motor, he cockily drove away.

"Oh! That *man*!" she exploded in exasperated laughter.

chapter

3

MORNING, AND APRIL, IN THE COUNTRY! After a phone call to establish that Gramps was still holding his own, Gypsy stood at the back porch rail and drank in the rich workings of earth, water, and light in the awakening land. She sighed, filled with pleasure, and lowered her vision to the hardy band of oaks that rambled down an incline to the backyard, mixing their distinctive musk with the pungent smell of the tillable acres off to the left. A movement, a slight rustle disturbing the silence at the edge of the woods, caught her notice: a white-tailed buck and three does drifted deeper into cover where they'd wait out the day before returning for nocturnal foraging in the Connor's unharvested cornfield bordering the trees. Illinois was the good life for deer with its fields rich with grain and patches of timber for shelter. Only a lengthy fall hunting season and a resurgence of the coyote population kept their numbers from posing a serious threat to the crops.

Gypsy smiled, unconsciously thanking God for creatures of such beauty. How she had missed mornings like this cramped in her city apartments. An old dream stirred in her, the one no one else guessed she cherished. Others seemed to assume that because Gypsy had wandered, she wanted to live that life always. Deep in her soul, she'd long nurtured a fantasy: some day, some spring, a handsome, successful, mysterious man would materialize at just the right moment ... he'd marry her ... they'd take up residence in a cozy country house to live surrounded by their strong, beautiful children—

You simpleton, she now scolded herself. Haven't you been around long enough to realize the unlikelihood of that scenario? Her smile twisted awry at the knowledge of how far most of her suitors to date had fallen short of her "dream" specifications. She sighed and sat down on the porch steps, noticing the touching vulnerability of swelling buds waiting everywhere to burst into leaves, flowers, grass. How trusting is nature, she marveled, always willing to renew one more time, to stake everything on the mercy of God's laws. When will I become that filled with faith? she pondered. Because right now, I can't lie, God. I can't say, "Not my will concerning Gramps, but Thine." Please, Lord, heal him. Let him come home to me.

Gypsy took from the pocket of her old fuzzy yellow bathrobe the card the hospital chaplain had given her yesterday when he'd stopped her in the hall for a moment's chat. She read aloud, "Now faith is being sure of what we hope for and certain of what we do not see." It was strange. Gramps, who was so sick—she had no doubt that he believed in what he couldn't see, in the goodness of all God's ways. But she, who was young, strong, healthy—did she?

Her questioning was cut short by the rumble of a car coming down the gravel lane from the main road. "Now, who . . . ?" she muttered, wondering if Dayt was back already with some more bossy instructions. He'd got the propane man out there by seven-thirty that morning. The racket had wakened her from a dead sleep. No doubt he'd be over to see that she followed his orders about the groceries, too.

She stood on tiptoe to peer over the bushes surrounding the porch. No, it wasn't Dayt's car. It was Aunt May's old green station wagon churning into the front drive like the dogged dinosaur it was.

"Good!" Gypsy murmured, and skipped down the steps and around the house to greet the beloved aunt extricating her short, rounded self, plus a wicker basket, from the "Green Machine," as her old boat was known.

"Aunt May, you're just in time for coffee! Come on in!" Gypsy hugged her aunt with one arm, taking the basket, redolent of something warm and yeasty, on the other.

"Well, now, I was counting on that, Gypsy, and I brought over a little something to go with it," Aunt May chirped in the soft confidentiality that marked all her conversation.

Aunt May always reminded Gypsy of a pretty little chipmunk, because to go with that brisk but murmurous voice she had deep brown hair, worn short and softly curled, huge, brown eyes that sparkled with fun, and full cheeks so naturally pink it was hard to believe they weren't painted.

"I made some coffeecake, caramel pecan; you always liked that, didn't you? I haven't had breakfast yet, have you? I just don't know where the time goes, Gypsy. One minute it's seven and I'm getting up, the next it's . . ." She took her arm from Gypsy's waist to consult her watch. "nine. I just don't know!"

All the while Aunt May chattered, she was bustling the two of them into the house and out to the kitchen with the peculiar, tiny-stepped gait that reinforced Gypsy's perception of her as a cuddly little animal.

The coffeecake oozed with Aunt May's typically luscious culinary touch, and the women, joined by a tousleheaded Jody, just out of bed, demolished nearly all of it and at the same time maintained a steady fire of catch-up talk. Aunt May was mother to six children: Tom, twenty, away at college; Sheila, eighteen, employed by the local bank; Randy, sixteen, and Jessica, fifteen, high-schoolers; Ruthie, ten, and Rachel, six, grade-schoolers. Her conversation was a blizzard of church and school events ranging from Promotion Sunday for Rachel's Sunday school class to Parent's Day at Tom's college. Gypsy was just pouring a third round of coffee when, over the raucous emanation from the living room TV, where Jody lay absorbing the Saturday morning cartoons, she heard another vehicle pull into the driveway. She scuffed, slipper-footed, to the dining room window to check.

"Oh, no!" she exclaimed at the sight of Dayt's maroon Corvette.

"Did you say something, dear?" Aunt May called from the kitchen.

"It's that smarty Dayton O'Rourke over here to bug me again," she complained, aware that she was still in her robe at ten-thirty in the morning, further evidence to him, she was sure, of her "laziness."

"What do you mean, 'bug' you?" Aunt May inquired,

scurrying up beside Gypsy to look out the window. "I've always thought Dayton was awfully nice—"

"Oh, it's just this power of attorney thing," Gypsy interjected. "He seems to think I'm some kind of flakehead and he's going to really straighten me out." She turned to face her aunt. "Do you know what he said to me last night? He said I was spoiled. And hot tempered. And lazy."

"O–oh . . . lazy? Why, Gypsy, you are certainly not lazy. No one in our family is lazy," Aunt May hedged.

"Why, I'm not spoiled, either! Am I?"

"Now, what's Dayt doing? Walking over to the barn?" Aunt May hurried to change the subject. "What would he be doing that for?"

Gypsy turned back to the window. Sure enough, Dayt was headed toward the barn, the famous Connor barn. Way back in the thirties, Gypsy's great-grandfather had been suddenly struck with a fever to build a livestock sale barn, cattle and hogs being major products of the Sauk Valley area. With the help of his neighbors, he'd designed and erected a huge, gambrel-roofed edifice of native oak, a building in many respects better built and maintained than either of the family residences. The sale barn venture had lasted about three years, and then the first Worthington Connor had lost interest in it just as fast as he'd become enamored of the project. But the barn, white, stately, and superior to every other building on the place, remained, an object of great pride to all the family even though its use devolved eventually into a simple storage shed.

Now Dayt's tall figure disappeared through a side door into the big building.

"What in the world is he snooping around there for?" Gypsy wondered aloud.

"Oh, I wouldn't call it snooping. Dayt's not the snoopy type, Gypsy," Aunt May said. "He's probably just checking it out to make sure it's all right. He knows how much it means to Dad Connor, you know."

Gypsy's reply was skeptical. "You're just seeing Dayt through rose-colored glasses, Aunt May. You never want to admit anyone's got bad motives, do you?" she accused affectionately.

"No," her aunt replied simply. "Besides, Worth just thinks the world of Dayton O'Rourke; says he's the most progressive farmer around, very conscious of soil conservation and all. Worth's very pleased that Dayton's taking care of Dad's affairs."

There was no use arguing with Aunt May, Gypsy knew, if Uncle Worth approved of Dayt. Worth's opinion might as well be carved in stone as far as his wife was concerned.

"I'm going to throw on some clothes. If Dayt comes to the house, entertain him a minute for me, will you?" she requested of her aunt.

"Surely, dear. Oh . . . and I ate the last of the coffeecake! What will I offer him with his coffee?"

Gypsy left her aunt worrying over that important matter and dashed into her room to pull on jeans and a sweater, then run a brush through her hair. When she came out, Dayt was politely accepting a cup of coffee from Aunt May, and Jody had deserted the TV to stand grinning shyly at his new friend.

"Hey, you're going to have to get up earlier than this, Sport, if you're going to be a farmer," Dayt kidded him. "It's nearly noon."

Jody colored; it was evident to Gypsy that he had a bad

case of hero worship going. If Dayt didn't approve of late sleeping—

"I saw you prowling around the barn, Dayt," she boldly interrupted, partly to relieve Jody's embarrassment. "Do you have special plans for it, too?" If Aunt May had heard his little play last night, joke though it was, she'd not think he's so great, Gypsy told herself. She's commented a few times about all those women who've gone in and out of his house over the years.

"Good morning Gypsy." Dayt turned a properly neighborly smile upon her. "As a matter of fact, I *was* inspecting it with an eye to some revamping. Mrs. Connor, may I sit down?" he inquired with such courtly good breeding that Aunt May twinkled as if he'd asked to kiss her hand.

"Oh, of course, Dayton! How thoughtless of me." Aunt May straightened her neat print wrap skirt in unconscious acknowledgement of Dayt's attractiveness.

People always agree with Dayt, Gypsy thought. They don't understand him the way I do.

"What is it you have in mind?" she inquired silkily. "Turning it into a . . . guesthouse, perhaps?" She noticed Jody's wary eye on the two of them. He apparently hadn't forgotten the fireworks of the night before.

Dayt's smile was naïve, irritatingly so. He sat at the big rectangular dining table, so the other three took seats there also. "What I have in mind is this: before Jesse got sick, he and I were negotiating for the lease of the barn."

"You mean Mike needs it, for storage or something?" Gypsy guessed.

"No, it wasn't for the use of O'Rourke Farms. It's . . . uh . . . for a summer theater."

45

A summer theater? The idea took Gypsy and her aunt so by surprise neither said a word.

"Let me go back to the beginning," he plunged on. "You see, an old friend of mine, my speech teacher back at St. Mark's High School, has worked on the side for years in professional theater, summer stock, dinner theater, that sort of thing. About two years ago, as part of a church project, she started an acting class and it just took off and zoomed. So she formed a semiprofessional company to do Christian theater. The players write a good deal of their own material and they take it around to church conventions, schools, retreats, just about anywhere in the Midwest they can afford to go for the minimal fee they charge."

Gypsy interposed, "What age are these actors? Adults? Teenagers?"

"Young adults. Most of them came under Ila's—-Ila Danova, that's my old teacher—under her tutelage at Bennington Christian College, where she now teaches. Anyway, they've been so successful that Ila wants to find a country place where they can light for a few months, work full-time to perfect their craft, teach, and perform naturally. Sort of a theater camp, you might say."

"Hmm. The Trapp Family Singers, except they're actors?" Gypsy wisecracked.

"Something like that. Ila will audition area youth who want to participate and pick about a dozen apprentices who'll pay tuition, of course."

"How did she happen to find out about our barn? Not that it doesn't have possibilities, now that I think of it."

"She spent a week at O'Rourke Farms last summer when she and some other friends came down for a rest. One look at Jesse's barn, and the idea for her theater camp was born."

"Oh. Well." Gypsy's thoughts were speeding a mile a minute. A Christian summer theater, right here in the Connor barn? That sounded exactly like the kind of thing a Connor would come up with—stimulating, innovative, and almost guaranteed not to be highly profitable. How had some stranger got ahead of them? "Well, tell me more, Dayt. How much would have to be done to the barn, and who would do it? Not to mention pay for it?"

"Really, not much would have to be changed structurally, and the work would be done by the troupe itself. We aren't talking about a sophisticated set-up, just one to serve the purpose of a very young, very flat-pursed company. The players will have to pay their own room and board, and . . . uh . . . the other expenses will be underwritten by private donors. With luck, the theater will take in enough to pay back the contributors. Some day."

Gypsy regarded Dayt with half-suspicious irony. "I don't suppose *you* know any of these *private donors* do you?"

His face darkened slightly, enough to tell her he was the underwriter. "Whoever they are, they're supporting a good thing," he assured her. "Ila Danova is one special teacher. She can draw the best out of a student without his even realizing it."

"That's wonderful, Dayton," Aunt May put in. "But somehow I'd never thought of religion and theater going together."

"It's a very old combination, Mrs. Connor. Ila's doctorate is in theater history. She says that back in the Middle Ages when few could read, Bible stories were often enacted as part of the church service. And the miracle and morality plays grew out of that into pageants that involved whole city populations. So theater has been a major factor in spreading the Christian message for a long time."

"That's kinda funny, isn't it?" Jody observed. "Goin' from the church to a barn?"

Dayt smiled, tolerant of the intrusion. "Well, Jody, Christianity was born in something pretty much like a barn, wasn't it?" He turned to the two women. "Why don't we go out to your barn, and I can show you what needs to be done?"

Jody scatted for his room to dress as Gypsy and Aunt May followed Dayt out to the big white building sitting a hundred yards from the house. Already Gypsy's mind was cataloging the possibilities. A parking lot in the cow pasture to the right of the barn, box office behind the split door leading to what had once been the sale barn office . . .

Dayt pushed open the great sliding doors that provided access to the roomy interior, and the three, plus a hastily attired Jody, stepped inside. The musty odor of old hay, old dust, and stale air enveloped them. In the broad center of the building were a hay rack and an ancient baler, stored there the previous fall, and the longer walls were banked with baled hay, disguising the concrete tiers where once sale barn patrons had sat on folding chairs to view the livestock paraded through the center for their inspection.

"Ila says this barn is a natural for theater-in-the-round. A low wooden platform in the center would serve as the stage, and a pipe grid could be hung from the rafters for the stage lights. At the far end, some simple partitions could provide dressing and storage rooms. We'd have to build a couple of wooden tiers at each end of the barn to make a true theater-in-the-round, but that wouldn't be a big project." Dayt swung around toward the other end. "Up here in the corner opposite the old sale barn office, we'd have to put in a small public restroom; that's a law. Also, the state building inspectors would have to be satisfied that there's no problem with exits or wiring. From what I've checked out, we're O.K. on both counts."

Gypsy viewed the area with new eyes. Could it be that the Connor barn was at last going to find a use suitably noble for its grand design? She was not a little intrigued with the idea.

"And you say Gramps was agreeable to all this?" she quizzed Dayt.

"Definitely. Jesse intended to sign the lease papers this weekend. Of course that's out now."

"Can't you sign them? I thought with power of attorney you could do just about whatever you wanted to with Gramps's property?" She deliberately needled him.

Dayt eyed her steadily. "I could, but I won't. We had no idea you were coming back here to live when we talked this out. You might find having a public attraction right on your doorstep to be a bit much."

Gypsy considered the situation in a mouth-puckered pose. "I don't know." She did, but why make it too easy for him? She relaxed her artificial "perplexed" expression. "I'm just an . . . 'entertainer' . . . remember? Not too stuffy to enjoy having something like this right under my nose."

Dayt's eyebrow arched, but before he could retort, Jody offered eagerly, "I like the idea, too, Gyps! Maybe we could set up a concession stand or somethin', make some mon—"

"Now, Jody, don't let your imagination run away with you," Gypsy warned. "Gramps may not want to go through with this now that he's sick. We'll just have to wait till he's well enough to make the decision."

"But don't you think it'd be fun?" Jody asked. "Maybe they'll need someone on keyboard and you won't have to be out on the road late nights, comin' home the way you were in New York."

"Aren't *you* the considerate one!" Gypsy grinned, ruffling Jody's crop of curls. "I think you've been bitten by the show biz bug, that's what I think."

Aunt May spoke up. "Dayton, are there enough people around here to support even a *little* theater?"

"Ila's researched that, too. We're about thirty miles from Peoria. Just a nice distance for a family or group out for an evening's fun not too far from home. The thing is, publicity would have to go into gear right away if we're going to carry this out. Ila wants to start the season the first of June and run till Labor Day."

For a few seconds the four of them stood looking at one another, then Gypsy broke the silence. "Well, I have no objections, if it's still agreeable with Gramps. I'll bring it up just as soon as I think he's ready for it."

"Yay! I bet he'll agree! I bet he'll like havin' some excitement around here, instead of just sittin' around listenin' to the crickets!" Jody chuckled. "You always said he likes fun and good times, Gypsy!"

The three adults laughed at Jody's boyish enthusiasm, and Gypsy realized he'd hit Gramps's nature pretty well for not knowing him.

"One thing, Dayt," she questioned when the laughter died down, "the troupe—how many are in it, and where will they stay? The motel in Sauk Valley?"

Dayt's hand rubbed the back of his neck, embarrassed. "You've hit a sore spot there, Gypsy. I . . . uh . . . assumed since there's only six permanent members, plus Ila, that they'd stay at my place. But when I mentioned it to Reva this morning, she blew her stack! Said she'd be nuts to play maid all summer to a bunch of actors!"

Reva was Mike Thompson's wife. The couple lived in the tenant house at O'Rourke Farms, and Reva took care of the cooking and housekeeping over at the big house whenever any O'Rourkes were there. A servant she was not.

A sickening-sweet, eye-batting smile cracked across Gypsy's face. "Why, Dayton, do you mean Reva has a tough, no-nonsense man like you intimidated?"

Dayt's baleful glare satisfied her urge to irk him, but his reply was smooth. "I'm not going to lose the best farmer I could have on my land just because his wife has a few . . . irritating peccadilloes. I know more than one woman with that problem, after all."

Gypsy took his return gibe with a smirky, tongue-in-cheek, "Oh?" that wheeled him abruptly to Aunt May.

"Well, it *would* be quite a lot for Reva to undertake," murmured that discreet peacemaker, "she not being used to children, even. If *I* had any room at all to offer—"

"Never, Mrs. Connor. You have all the work you need with that beautiful big family you've got," Dayt averred. "But thank you, anyway."

Aunt May's cheeks grew even pinker at the flattering reference to her brood. "You know I'd like to help you out, Dayt, being neighbors and all. Why couldn't I inquire around, see if there isn't someone, maybe in my church circle, willing to board a few extra for the summer?"

"*Would* you, Mrs. Connor? That would be a tremendous load off my back," Dayt said, relieved. "There *is* one other little matter. The apprentices will have to be fed a light supper on performance nights. There won't be time for them to go into town to eat. We were hoping whoever kept the troupe would feed the apprentices, too."

"I think that could be worked out, Dayton. Perhaps some kind of box lunch, delivered here early in the evening, or something," Aunt May thought aloud. The chug of an old tractor broke in on the conversation. "Oh, that must be Worth. He wanted to get to that stand of corn south of your house, Gypsy. He got so involved with Jake Low's fall harvest—Jake fell and broke his hip, you know—he never did finish our own corn picking."

By the time the four got to the big door, Uncle Worth was hoisting his stocky frame off the tractor. He took after his mother's people, being tall, big-boned, and light-haired. He and Aunt May made an incongruous couple as she skittered to his side just like a newlywed, but Gypsy saw the halo of love and respect that gave their marriage a glow to be envied by pairs far more glamorous.

"Dayt! Good to see you!" Uncle Worth called out, shaking hands with his sometime neighbor. "Gyps." He had a kiss for her. He blessed Jody with a fatherly pat on the shoulder. "Dayt, you're just the man I want to see. I've been in touch with the Northern Regional Research Center at Peoria and they're willing to help us with our plans to get prairie grass started in our waterways. They're sending out a team to look things over and make recommendations next week." Uncle Worth and Dayt moved over to lean against the wagon while they continued their discussion over the roar of the idling tractor.

"What's so special about prairie grass, Gyps?" Jody wanted to know.

"It's native grasses, Big Blue Stem, Switch Grass, Indian Grass." Aunt May volunteered. "Used to cover this state so high the first pioneers couldn't see over it, even on horseback. They had to climb trees to see ahead and use a compass so as not to get lost."

"But what would anyone want of it now?"

"It's the best natural defense against soil erosion known to man," Aunt May continued, enthusiastic over a topic dear to Worth's heart, and therefore hers. "And they're even experimenting to find a way to make it palatable feed for livestock. All the buffaloes lived on it, but of course, they're more noted for their tough constitutions than their tender steaks."

"Now we both know about prairie grass," Gypsy remarked to Jody. For having grown up on a farm, she knew little about agriculture. Music and gypsies, and dreaming—those had been her youthful interests.

"Oh, dear, I do sound . . . professorial . . . don't I, when I get started on conservation!" Aunt May chuckled, merry in her apology. "Well, anyway, Jody, that's why Dayton and Worth are going to experiment with prairie grass." She glanced at her watch. "Goodness! I've got to get home and put lunch on the table. Dayton," she called as he and Uncle Worth broke up their conversation, "I'll be in touch about a place for those actors. If worse comes to worst, I just know we can find room for them at our house."

"If worse comes to worst, Mrs. Connor, they can stay at my place. They can fend for themselves, and we'll leave Reva out of it." His words were brave, but Gypsy thought they sounded a trifle defensive. It tickled her to no end that he couldn't bulldoze the redoubtable Reva.

"Well, if you say so. . . ." Aunt May bid them all farewell, and soon her Green Machine lumbered off for home. Uncle Worth swung up onto the tractor seat and gunned the vehicle to snorting life, bound for a job eight months delayed.

Dayt watched them leave, and Gypsy could tell by the kind but amused lines about his mouth he was thinking, If only Worth and May worked as hard for themselves as they do for others. . . . Instead of saying it aloud, he turned to Jody. "How would you like to go over to O'Rourke Farms with me for the rest of the day? If you're interested, I think I've got some summer jobs you could handle."

"Yeah?" Jody replied, pricking up his ears. "Sure, Dayt. Glad to help you out." Neither Dayt nor Gypsy reacted by a flicker to the crack in his voice that rather diluted his manly response. "I'll . . . uh . . . wait in the car," he threw out offhandedly, and stalked over to get into the Corvette with all the cool he could muster, remarkably imitative of Dayt's easy grace.

"What a chameleon!" Gypsy laughed, shaking her head. "The first thing I know, he'll be a Chicago lawyer!" She turned serious. "What kind of work do you have in mind for him, Dayt?"

"Mainly lawn mowing and cleanup around the farm. He could bring the mower over here and do your yard, too. I'll pay him minimum wage."

Gypsy didn't say anything for a moment. It would be a godsend to have Jody occupied with something worthwhile, and as to the money—well, she wasn't going to have much to share with him. Still, it gave her a funny feeling the way the ties between her family and Dayt seemed to be multiplying.

"It—it would be good for him, I'm sure," she forced herself to say. "But he's spent an awful lot of his life in front of TV. You'd have to teach him how to work."

"I figured that. But he's going to grow up really fast, Gyps. This is the time for him to learn that a man pays his own way."

What could she say? That was exactly the way she'd been brought up, so how could she say, "Sorry, I don't want so many links to you"?

"Thanks, then." She paused; it had to be said. "But I think you'd better understand: Jody's never had a father. I think he's going to get very attached to you. . . ."

"Yes?" Dayt inquired when she failed to finish the sentence.

She faced him squarely. "If he does, are you going to . . . laugh . . . at him, too?"

A dark edge of color seeped under Dayt's cheekbones; his eyes became sabers, slicing into hers. "All right, Miss Prissy Prue, let's get this straight once and for all." His stone-hard grasp pulled her back from the doorway, into the barn where Jody couldn't see them. "I'm tired of your accusing me of some kind of animal attack on your virtue! In the first place, Jody is a boy, not a pretty little teenage girl batting her eyes at me over a punch glass, so the case isn't the same at all. *He* wants to learn to be a man. *You* were using me to prove you were a woman."

"That's *not* so! That's the biggest lie—" Gypsy could hardly speak over her angry hurt.

"No, Gypsy. The lie is what you've been telling yourself, that you didn't ask for exactly what you got, a rattling good kissing session with a man gentleman enough to stop before you got a whole lot more than you were bargaining for."

"*You*? A gentleman? Don't make me laugh!" Gypsy snapped sarcastically. "So you didn't actually throw me down and—"

She stopped, flung into the memory of that long, hot summer when Dayt had suddenly seen her as more than "the little neighbor girl." The O'Rourkes had just put in a pool; he'd taught her to swim, laughed and made jokes with her, wrapped her heart in an infatuation that had racked her with longing. Then came the O'Rourkes' anniversary fete. Giddy with her first big, sparkly party, she'd let him dance her off into a dark corner; all at once he was kissing her with a reckless passion that had left her breathless, tore at her defenses until she crashed the barrier and gave back fire for fire.

In a moment of regained sanity, they'd broken apart, stared at each other, then she was running, scared by desire intense beyond her imaginings. Followed by laughter. *His* laughter.

She drew in a breath, hiding the jagged wound that ached as searingly today as it had five years before. "You led me on; you let me develop the last full-blown crush of my teen years—" Her throat constricted, but she managed to finish. "—and then you laughed at me for giving in to it." The accusation stood alone in the air, ugly and painful.

Something moved in his sea-storm eyes; shame replaced anger. "Gypsy. . . ." He hesitated, then went on. "I was a jerk to laugh. You want an apology, you've got it. I was a jerk."

His ready admission of guilt left her without a comeback; she hadn't expected it.

"I was coming off the losing end of a long relationship that summer; I was looking around for something to lift me out of the dumps, and every time I came home, here was this cute little Gypsy, the girl I'd watched grow up, hanging around, trying out her sexual wings on the only man in the county not already in love with her—"

"I was *not* hanging around! Your folks were always inviting me over to play the piano or swim, and you know it!"

"Okay, okay," he soothed. "At any rate, you were around a lot, and you were fun. And you had a string of boyfriends a mile long chasing after you. I thought you just wanted to add an older man to your list of conquests, and I was the one you'd picked. I thought it was a game, and I'd won."

"A game? I don't play that kind of game, Dayt."

"You mean you actually took me seriously?" His brows knit in concern. "Honey, a girl of nineteen, a man of thirty—they're not quite in the same world. I'd been involved—very much so—with a grown-up woman; I wasn't—I'm not the cradle-robbing type."

Gypsy couldn't let him know how much he'd meant to her, couldn't bare her foolish teenage daydreams to his scrutiny, so she said, "I realize that now, Dayt. Now that I'm a grownup too. But at the time, I was scalded alive." She laughed mirthlessly. "Kids recover quickly, though, don't they? I can't believe how silly I was, now."

They stood face to face, each assessing the other's

57

sincerity. If he was telling the truth about an unhappy love affair, then Gypsy could at least understand his behavior, even if she couldn't excuse it. Hadn't she heard a hundred such tales of romantic woe from young men draped over her keyboard, bending her sympathetic ear?

"Well." She dropped her eyes. "I guess it's all water under the bridge, isn't it? I'm no longer an impressionable teenager, and you're . . . maybe . . . a little kinder?" She stepped back, and his hands dropped slowly from her shoulders.

"I hope so, Gypsy. I want to be." The soft husk in his voice gave her heart a little twist. Maybe it was better to fight with him, spare herself the misery of seeing his good side. She didn't *dare* to like him.

"Well!" She straightened briskly. "I've got a full day's activity to carry out, and only half a day to do it in. It's going to take me a while to adjust to daylight working hours! Will you excuse me, please?"

"Sure, Gyps. And, once again, I'm sorry for laughing at you. I guess that's what happens when you're so sorry for yourself you don't think of other's feelings, isn't it? What do you say we start all over, as business partners this time? Maybe that'll keep us from chewing each other up?"

He wanted to be friends, she could tell from the warmth in his eyes. She considered. Really, what choice did she have?

"All right. Strictly business, that's you and me." Her heart wasn't as confident as her words.

Gypsy's first priority of the afternoon was to visit Gramps at the hospital in Shawana, the county seat. Her hopes soared with her first glance into the coronary unit; Gramps was alert and able to speak for his few allotted minutes before a nurse signaled Gypsy it was time to leave. Just seeing the life returning to Gramps's usually vital frame told Gypsy as much as the nurse's low-voiced report: he seemed to have passed the crisis. Another day or two and he could be moved to a regular hospital room. Gypsy's murmured prayers of thanks lasted all the way back to Sauk Valley, where she headed for the Market Basket to reap a much-needed harvest from the store's crowded shelves.

Sauk Valley was just a village, population twelve hundred, so her foraging was halted frequently by long-time friends wanting to know how Gramps was doing and how she felt to be back in her old hometown. Gypsy knew that to many Sauk Valleyans she was a curiosity. Not many local girls went traipsing off across the country to make music to eat dinner by. Still, the questions were kindly, and she was feeling so good about Gramps that she lingered unhurriedly over the many conversations.

By the time she got home, unloaded a heaping shopping cart's worth of groceries, and put supper on the table, Jody was back, chock-full of news about his first day on a farm. Gypsy had to suppress a laugh. He might be trying to walk and talk like Dayt when the Revered One was around, but his tone-downed verbal exuberance fled like the wind once he was alone with "good old Gyps." He had to let out his discoveries or burst!

"Dayt's farm is really neat, isn't it, Gypsy? He doesn't have any barn, just metal buildings. He says barns are a thing of the past; farm buildings today have to hold machinery, like his big Steiger tractor. And hay isn't stored inside anymore. He showed me huge rolls of it out in his fields and said they weighed about a ton apiece! And his cattle—did you know he's got over five hundred head of cattle?—not one of them is a milker; they all turn into beefsteak." Jody hardly took notice of the food set before him.

Gypsy poked him to gain his attention. "Have a pork chop or three, Jody, and pass me the potatoes, please."

"Oh, sure." Heaping mashed potatoes onto his already crowded plate, Jody continued his monologue. "Dayt took me into town for lunch. Boy, Sauk Valley is really small, isn't it? Like Dayt says, you could fit the whole population into one good-sized high-rise like we have in Chicago or New York. Could I have another muffin, please, Gyps? They're really good!"

"That depends. Do I hear a note of condescension toward my hometown from a big city dude?" she teased.

"No way, Gyps. Dayt likes Sauk Valley. Says the best time of his childhood was what he spent at O'Rourke Farms."

"In that case—" She passed him the covered basket and watched with satisfaction as he broke open a steaming blueberry muffin that met with his deepest approval. There was something kind of pleasing about filling up, or rather, *trying* to fill up, a teenage boy.

"You know the business proposition Dayt said he had for me?"

Gypsy nodded yes, wondering how many more times she was going to hear "Dayt says" before the evening was out.

"He wants me to clean up his house and barnyards, and then keep them mowed all summer. He's got a riding mower that looks like a midget tractor. Man! Has it got power! And he's gonna pay me, too. Minimum wage. 'Course, I'll have to pull some weeds by hand, up close to the buildings, but mostly I'll be on that old tractor, makin' the grass fly!"

"Now, Jode," Gypsy warned, "I don't think Dayt's hiring you to tear up his lawn *or* his mower."

"Don't worry, Gyps. Dayt says. . . ."

Oh, it's going to be a long night, Gypsy moaned inwardly. Dayt says. . .Dayt says. . .Dayt says. . . .

chapter
4

"HELLO, GRAMPS!" Gypsy's greeting was soft and happy. She hastened from the doorway to the hospital bed to take the hand of the small, dark, wiry man cranked up to a half-sitting position.

"Gypsy!" Gramps's face wreathed in the fond smile of a doting grandparent. "I was hoping you'd come by before I dropped off to sleep again. Doggone! I just can't seem to keep my eyes open more than five minutes at a time!"

"Well, don't you fight it, Gramps. You need a lot of rest, you know, so you can get out of here and come home where you belong." Gypsy drew a chair close to his bed, never letting go of the warm, dry hand, knotted with years of work, that felt like all she knew of parental love.

"Yes. Yes, I want to go home, honey. Wherever that may be."

"Why—you know where your home is, Gramps," she replied, puzzled. Had some medication confused his ordinarily sharp intellect? Then she saw in the depths of his eyes a smile, different, as if from a distance.

Gramps laid his other hand atop hers and patted gently. "Sure I do, Gyps. Don't worry, your old grandpappy isn't losing his mind," he comforted, guessing her fear, "just waxing philosophical. The past ten days—well, sometimes I feel like I've been on a long journey, Gyps, right to the outskirts of my heavenly home. 'Least I *hope* it'll be heaven!" he added in mild jesting.

"Oh, Gramps, don't you talk that way! You're going to recover completely; the doctor says so. He says you're almost out of the woods." Gypsy squeezed his hand in her fervor to will him to good health.

"Well, Doc knows best, doesn't he?" Gramps shifted on the raised bed. "How does it feel to be back in the old house again, Gypsy?" His warm eyes searched her face.

"Good, Gramps!" she answered vehemently. Quick guilt splashed her. "I don't know now how I stayed away for five years; I shouldn't have. I should have come home now and then instead of expecting you to come visit me—"

"Now, Gyps, don't you ever blame yourself for that," Gramps broke in. "You had so little time off. Besides," he chuckled, "I liked coming out to visit you. Gave me an excuse to go traipsing with a clear conscience. We had some good times, didn't we, honey? Remember the week I spent with you in Boston? Worth a college education, that was."

"That *was* fun, Gramps. We'll do it again some day, too."

He didn't answer; instead, he continued smiling at his beloved grandchild and stroking her hand as if to soak up as much of her love as he could. Finally he said, "How's the boy doing? Getting used to life in the country?"

"He seems to be adjusting pretty well. I got him enrolled in Sauk Valley High, and he came home all astonished. Said there were only half as many in the whole school as there'd been in his ninth grade class back in New York City. But I guess he's finding out kids are still kids, no matter where they are."

"That's true; that's true. I noticed he talked a lot about Dayt that afternoon you brought him to meet me."

Gypsy stirred in her chair. "Yes, he . . . uh . . . well, Dayt has gone out of his way to be nice to him, and Jody is just eating it up. He's never had a father figure, you know." She shifted again uneasily. "Gramps, I want you to know, just as soon as I can, I'll get work. I don't expect you to support me, let alone my little stray."

"Gypsy." Gramps leaned forward, intense. "You did right to come home; you did right to bring the boy. You'll never regret it either, mark my words. It's right for a family to come together when trouble strikes any one member. It's right to take in the orphan and give him a home. And it's right for me to help the two of you all I can. When you get to the end of your days, you'll be glad for everything you ever did that made someone else's life a little better." He settled back, tired by the sudden burst of feeling. "Love for others—and what they have for you—it'll be the only thing that counts, honey, the only thing."

Tears rose in Gypsy's eyes. She didn't cry easily, but her grandfather's words touched to the core of her tender heart. "Oh, Gramps," she whispered over the lump in her throat, "you're not at the end of your days, but I'll tell you one thing: you and Grandma have done so much for me! There have been so many times when I've been protected from bad choices because you and Grandma showed me by your lives how I ought to live. I love you, Gramps! I love you." She laid her face against his hand, and the tears fell to wet his arm. If only, if *only* she could pour her youth and strength into him! He, who had always been so joyously full of living, why now did he somehow seem so *above* life?

"I've been a very lucky man, Gypsy," Gramps said, throat clogged with his own emotion. "I was born to a good family, married to the sweetest woman in the world, raised two fine sons, and lived to see grandchildren to do any man proud. When Catherine died—for awhile I thought God was being mean to me. But now I know, just as sure as I'm lying here like a regular old loafer, that we'll always be together, the whole family, one way or another. You hold on to that, Gyps."

Gypsy fought down the sorrow that wanted to swamp her until she was able to promise, "I will, Gramps." She began to swab her eyes with a tissue and straightened up, resolved to get this conversation back on a lighter track. "Well." She blew her nose, then said brightly, "I can't wait for you to see the house, Gramps. Aunt May has been helping me get it all spruced up."

Gramps' black eyebrows twitched with the humorous quirk that always made Gypsy giggle. "Why, I've been living with the dust of that house so long we're old friends. And I'll bet I won't be able to find a blamed thing, will I? You'll have everything all fancied up like Worth and May's home, with quilts and plants and gee-gaws tripping me up every which way."

"That's just what we've done," Gypsy teased, delighted with the return to his oldtime raillery. "Your old recliner chair? We covered that with pink calico and put a big white ruffle around the foot rest."

"I don't doubt it for a minute! What about my work

shoes? I don't suppose they dare sit right by my chair where I can get at 'em first thing in the morning, do they?" Gramps inquired facetiously.

"Oh, Aunt May made them into the cutest planters—filled them with dirt and put in petunias!" Gypsy assured him.

Gramps's laugh echoed his former merriment. The talk drifted from there to the dozens of ordinary tidbits that make up family conversation. Gypsy decided today was the day to bring up the barn lease.

"Gramps, several days ago Dayt informed me that you were about to lease the barn for a summer theater before you got sick. Do you still want to go through with it?"

"How do you feel about it, Gyps? Do you mind?"

"My only concern is that the hubbub will be too much for you. You'll need a lot of rest, you know."

Gramps's gaze was clear and firm. "I'll get my rest, honey, all I need. I really want that barn to be used for the Lord's work."

Gypsy pulled the form from her purse and handed it to her grandfather, then scrounged up a pen. He read the document carefully and affixed his signature.

"Gyps, I know that a few years ago you and Dayt had some kind of tiff, but for your sake, I want you to get along with him. He's a good man, a decent man, different from us Connors, it's true; he's got a knack for making money. But there's nothing wrong with that if that's where your interests and talents lie and you do it honestly. When I'm gone, half the farm will go to you. Your mom and dad wanted it that way. Worth and I agree: Dayt's the man to oversee your farming business until such time he deems you capable of handling it yourself."

Gypsy felt her blood pressure take off for the moon! Tied to Dayton O'Rourke until *he* deemed her fit to run her own affairs? How could Gramps do this to her?

"I can see the fire shooting out of your eyes, but tell me how much you know about the actual managing of a farm?"

"We—well," she stuttered. "I grew up on one; I know what goes on—"

"In a general way, you do. But it's like Dayt says, the days of hit-or-miss farming, 'least in Illinois, are over. You've got to know everything from accounting to basic science, then be able to apply it all in the pure, physical labor of farming. See, the difference between Worth and me, and Dayt and Mike Thompson, is that they put into practice all the things Worth and I know ought to be done, but just don't get around to. So until you learn all you need to know and then find someone to do the actual labor, you're a hundred times better off letting Dayt make the decisions. Frankly, I expect that Worth will turn his farming over to Dayt and Thompson once I'm gone, so he can go into full-time teaching. And he ought to. Worth's got the reputation of a topnotch teacher, and he's only stuck around the farm 'cause he knows I can't go it alone. His boys both want to go into medicine, so there's no reason to stay on the land for their sakes."

Dayt says, Dayt says—Gypsy controlled her impatience with that expression, knowing that she had no business vexing Gramps with her doubts about Dayton O'Rourke's "nobility," but she couldn't resist one mild objection. "I never thought, Gramps, you'd want to see anyone but Connors on Connor land. You know if Dayt runs it long enough, he'll want to buy it, and then the farm will be just one more acreage in his fiefdom."

Gramps laughed outright, then got serious. "Listen to yourself, Gypsy. You know as well as I do, the O'Rourkes are good people, and they don't hold any 'fiefdom.' Land should belong to those who know how to use it, not abuse it. No Connor ever overworked his land, that's for sure, and if it turns out to be the O'Rourkes, so be it. Do you think the Lord worries about who owns a patch of land for a few paltry years?"

That was as close to a chastening as Gypsy had ever got from Gramps. She desisted immediately in her protests. "No, I guess not, Gramps. But you didn't really think I'd submit to some man's domination without a little bit of fight, did you?"

His laughter warmed her heart like wine. "Oh, Gyps, I've got a feeling you and Dayt as business partners—that will be a mighty entertaining spectacle! Between the two of you, there's enough ego to set off your own electrical storm!"

"And just what does that mean?" she challenged, grinning.

"Just the mutterings of an old man," he grinned. "Just the mutterings of an old man."

Gypsy stood in the middle of the living room and surveyed it with satisfaction. It wasn't grand, but it was far more cheery and fresh than it had been last Friday when she'd returned from New York. Elbow grease and imagination—they'd done wonders for the succession of dreary furnished apartments she'd occupied over the past five years, and they'd done the trick here, too. She and Aunt May had cleaned and rearranged, accenting the good antiques and hiding a plentitude of shabby upholstery under some K-Mart-special terry cloth in rust and peach, bringing a semblance of unity to the formerly lawless color scheme. Rooting around in the attic, they'd found some of Grandma's crocheted rag rugs, and these, plus a tough, colorful Indian rug some traveling Connor had brought back from the Southwest, disguised the various holes in the worn brown carpet covering the dining and living room floors. Aunt May had donated generously from her forest of healthy houseplants, and Gypsy had repotted them in interesting containers ranging from an eight-gallon stone crock to an ancient coal bucket.

The kitchen, too, met with her approval; it positively shone after a scrub-down and a perk-up with bright yellow print curtains Aunt May ran up from some cheap bed sheets. Aunt May was a whiz at the sewing machine.

Gypsy sat down at the sadly out-of-tune piano and riffed a few chords, then swung into a zippy number, the kind Gramps had always loved to hear after a day's work. She didn't know the name of it; it was something she'd picked up on the car radio coming home from the hospital, and it suited her mood perfectly. Gramps was going to be home again, she knew he was.

Rap! Rap! Rap! The old iron doorknocker startled her. She hadn't heard a car come down the drive. She went to the door, peering cautiously out of a dining room window before opening it. It was Dayt. She looked at her watch. He must have left Chicago right after lunch to get here by three. She took a deep breath. I will be pleasant to him, she vowed, for Gramps' sake.

"Look what the cat dragged in." The teasing insult leaped out even as she pulled open the door and stepped aside to welcome him. She was always a little surprised by the size of the man; his golden head barely cleared the doorframe.

"He's better, huh?" Dayt guessed.

"How did you know that?" Gypsy asked. It was uncanny, not to say uncomfortable, the way he seemed to zero in on her thoughts and moods.

"'Cause you're skinny and sassy, Squirt," Dayt teased, tweaking her nose. "You go formal when you're mad or down in the dumps."

"Hmf!" She walked over to the table and turned, grinning. "Well, you're right. For once. And I have something for you." She opened her purse and handed him the signed barn lease.

"Well, good girl." He unzipped his jacket, not waiting for her invitation to stay awhile. "The work crew, which is also the stage crew, light crew, and company of actors, should be down here by next weekend to start the renovation. Has Mrs. Connor got them a place to stay yet?"

"She's still working on it. The problem is, Dayt, that a lot of people assume all actors are, shall we say, a bit on the eccentric side. They're a little reluctant to bring them right under their own roof. But never fear, Aunt May will come up with something."

"Mmm. Well, I hope so. I can't say I especially want them running amok at my house either, but in a pinch—"

"For *Ila* you'd do it, wouldn't you?" Somehow she found his affectionate respect for his old teacher amusing.

As a schoolboy, he had probably been Ila's worst discipline problem.

"That's right, I would. So make something of that, Small fry."

"Don't you know it's rude to make fun of a woman's appearance?" she kidded.

He chortled. "I haven't met a woman yet who minded being called 'small' or 'thin.' You've all got a phobia on the subject."

"In that case, I won't offer you some of the apple-spice cake I just took out of the oven. I'd have to join you, and I don't want to get fat."

He seated himself at the big oak table. "Bring it on, Missy; I'm starved. I skipped lunch because I wanted to get down here with a proposition for you before some other lucky dude beats me to it."

She turned, halfway to the kitchen, hand on hip, and gave him a dirty look. "Haven't you learned? I'm not in the market for 'propositions'."

"You'd better hear what it is first," he returned, unabashed. "I have to run down to Peoria to pick up some special seed corn we're going to plant tomorrow. I thought maybe you and Jody would like to ride along and have dinner down there, if you don't mind riding in a pickup truck, that is. That's to make up for the dinner I cadged off you last weekend."

"Oh. You don't have to make up for that," she replied, not wanting his forced gratitude. "After all, you're paying for the food we eat, anyway, aren't you?" She had to get in that dig.

He rose from the table and stalked over to her, towering

over her with the easy arrogance of a man powerful in body and confidence, but she refused to back off. "You'd better get that cake in here, pronto, if you don't want your boy to come home and find his 'mommy' getting her bottom whacked, the way it should have been about twice a day when she was a spoiled child."

"*You* have got some crazy ideas about how to treat a woman, haven't you?" she scoffed, knowing his threat of physical violence was just talk. "You can just come off that 'Keep 'em barefoot and pregnant' jazz with me, buster!"

"Yeah?" He bent over her, hands hooked on pockets, taunting her with his amused condescension. "I don't think you've got the faintest idea of how I *want* to treat a woman—we're not talking about spoiled brats here, but a *woman*—"

"Phoo! That's not the half of it. I don't *care* how—"

"Well, you're going to hear it anyway, Smarty-pants. I *want* to treat a woman with respect; I want to love her and encourage her and protect her. If that makes me some kind of chauvinist pig—tough shooting!"

They stood nose to nose, glaring and giggling at each other's adamance until the whine of a school bus coming to a halt at the end of the lane ended their stand-off.

The pickup rumbled importantly across the thirty mile stretch of Illinois prairie separating Sauk Valley from Peoria, that most misunderstood of American cities. Inside, three rollicking companions chorused the last lines of the ditty issuing from the radio.

"Hey, we're pretty good!" Gypsy announced. "Let's all three go on the road for Matt Morris. What'll we call ourselves?"

Because Gramps was so much improved today, because Jody's angular boy-face was wreathed in grins, because she was young and healthy and full of life, Gypsy was on top of the world. For a few hours she intended to throw worry to the winds and be a girl again.

"How about 'The Three Stooges'?" Dayt suggested. "I get to be Moe."

Jody let loose with a round-eyed "Mee-mee-mee-meep!" that perfectly incarnated Curly, the hairless Stooge.

"No!" Gypsy cried over her laughter. "Let's be 'Laurel and Hardy Plus One'! I just crack up every time Stan says, 'A fine mess you've got us into this time, Ollie!'"

"I thought he said, 'Well, *this* is a fine kettle of fish!'" Dayt corrected, chuckling.

"Uh . . . uh! You're both wrong," Jody insisted. "It's 'Another fine mess you've got us into *this* time, Stanley.' Hardy says it. I know; I've seen them a hundred times on the old movies!" He could have been the rotund Oliver Hardy, so well did Jody's voice mimic the great comedian.

The truck cab rang with good-natured laughter as the riders argued about who said what. Gypsy's ease came partly from knowing she looked good. The desperate juggling of bath, shampoo, blow drying, and make-up following Dayt's invitation for dinner had culminated in a face cover-girl lovely and hair that cascaded like spun satin to her shoulders. She was wearing her new silver-gray spring suit with a ruffly soft violet blouse that matched her eyes; her shoes were dainty silver-gray sandals. She thought she looked good, and Dayt's blue-green appraisal of her before leaving had confirmed it.

It was fun to ride in the high, bouncy pickup and look

down upon motorists in mere cars. The incongruity of the well-dressed trio buzzing along in a truck suited her off-beat Connor taste. Of one thing she was sure, Dayt could come into town in a buckboard wagon and nobody would mistake him for an "uncouth rustic." In his dark blue tweed jacket and navy trousers, white silk shirt and maroon pin-dotted ascot, he looked his usual casually correct self, handsome enough to take the eye of any woman.

"How come the farmers along here aren't chisel plowing, Dayt?" Jody asked, gazing out at the conventionally furrowed fields being worked. "I thought you said chisel plowing left enough corn stalks and stuff to help hold the land in place, not let it blow away." Jody was rapidly becoming an expert on farming methods.

"This land is too flat for that kind of tillage, Jody. If we should have a rainy growing season, the extra residue would hold in too much water and drown the plants. It works best on slightly hilly ground like we have around Sauk Valley. It's just another one of the tightropes farmers constantly walk between what's best for the land and what's good for crop production."

Jody meditated that bit of new knowledge until they reached the outskirts of Peoria, whereupon he posed another question. "Is this the Peoria the comedians and politicians all joke about; you know, 'How will it play in Peoria?' Why do they say that?"

Dayt laughed. "Because it's not Chicago."

"Hoo hah!" Gypsy interrupted. "It's because back in the days of vaudeville, performers used to try out new routines in Peoria, as its population was considered relatively normal, unlike some others we could name."

"Oh, yeah?" Dayt shot back. "Well, I'll have you know Peoria and Chicago have a lot in common, only Peoria's just a pee-wee city, about 130,000 people. Both cities grew out of the travels of the great French explorers, Joliet and Marquette, in 1673. Both cities became incorporated towns in the 1830's. And they both have Indian names."

"But Peoria was the first permanent white village in Illinois, and its French background is as strong as that of New Orleans. Furthermore, the inhabitants got along peaceably with their Indian neighbors, the Potawatomis, Sac, and Fox. Not many communities can say that."

"Are there any Indians living around here now?" Jody inquired.

"Nope," Dayt said. "They've gone like the prairie grass."

"You said Chicago and Peoria are both Indian names, Dayt. What do they mean?"

"Oh, I'm glad you asked that, Jode!" Gypsy grinned. "Peoria means 'Beautiful View.' Tell him what Chicago means, Professor Moe," she demanded.

"Well . . . uh . . . I don't just recall—" Dayt fudged.

"It means, Jody, 'Place of the Skunk,' *or* 'Wild Onion.' In other words . . . Chicago stinks!" Gypsy crowed. "And, oh, yes, a further star for Peoria: Abraham Lincoln and Stephen Douglas had their first debate right here in li'l ol' pee-wee Peoria!"

"Some day," Dayt said as he leaned over to Jody, "I'll take you to Chicago and you can see a *real* city, the most exciting one in the United States, if you want to know the truth."

"But not nearly so big as New York City, is it?" Jody earned himself Dayt's fake-mean stare with his gibe.

Then they were within the city built on the bluffs of the Illinois River, headed down to a warehouse on the waterfront. After picking up the seed corn, Dayt took them to River Station, a former Rock Island Line rail depot converted into an impressive restaurant. The grandeur of turn-of-the-century taste lingered in great leaded glass windows, high ceilings, brass work, and heavy dark wood. Throughout the leisurely meal, Dayt and Gypsy talked barn theater while Jody devoted himself mainly to vacuuming in vast amounts of the delicious fare. At length he excused himself to roam the premises and inspect memorabilia of a bygone era.

Dayt settled in his chair and regarded Gypsy over the candlelight. He didn't speak. She sipped her coffee, studied her nails, glanced around at her fellow diners, anything to avoid the steady surveillance from across the table. Finally she met his gaze. "Is there something wrong? Have I got butter on my chin, or something?"

Dayt chuckled, deep and taunting, and his aquamarine eyes danced with speculative humor. "Your chin's perfect. You're a good-looking woman, Gypsy. You must have been told that a lot in the past five years."

Her silky brows raised. "I've been told in the past few days that I'm skinny. You, obviously, prefer voluptuosity."

"*Voluptuosity?* Is that a word?" He laughed outright. His eyes appraising her, he said, "I prefer women who understand their individual style and make the most of it. That suit does nice things for you, fills you out and softens you. Makes me forget that sharp temper you keep honed."

"*Really?* Well, I'm so glad I please you, Mr. O'Rourke. Tell me, when does your new list of best-and-worst dressed women come out?" She was peeved at his personal comments, yet flattered that he considered her good-looking.

He grinned mischievously, openly enjoying her half-irritated spunkiness. "The next time I think your appearance bears remarking upon." He leaned forward to sip the last of his coffee. "What has life been like for you since you left Sauk Valley, Mary Catherine?" The jesting was replaced with seriousness.

Brooding, Gypsy circled the rim of her water glass with one finger. "Well—" How much should she tell him? Only the good times? Or dare she trust him with the lesser moments, the hours when she'd longed to trade places with one of the oh-so-in-love girls she sometimes saw dabbling at the food and casting flirty, candlelighted glances at her lover?

"It was interesting one hundred percent of the time. You see miniature dramas played out right before your eyes. But I got tired too. Especially on nights when all the requests were for songs I don't particularly like! I'd say the whole experience was . . . educational."

He sat silently a moment. Then he asked, "And men? Did you learn not to run away?"

It wasn't an idle question, but did he deserve to know? And why did he care? She answered honestly, "I didn't put myself into situations where I had to make that decision."

"Oh." That was all he said, but she saw something akin to relief pass through his eyes before he dropped them and came round to help her out of her chair. "I see Jody's finished his tour of the building, so I suppose we'd better go. I've got to be out in the field by five in the morning, and we old men can't take late hours."

Gypsy stood, leisurely. This was a chance she couldn't pass. "I wonder how *I'll* feel when I'm middle-aged? Slowed down? Full of wisdom? Like you?"

A tongue-in-cheek grin accompanied Dayt's eyebrow-cocked survey. "You really know how to hurt a guy, Gyps!"

"Well, you're the one who's always bringing up our age difference. I was just . . . wondering."

"Do you really think I'm too old for you?" he inquired, not altogether facetiously.

She thought it over. "It's not easy to say. It's a possibility, of course. But then, women are known to mature much faster than men. *Much* faster."

"Yeah? Depends."

"On what?"

"Some women are childish at thirty; some are mature at eighteen. I guess it depends on what the woman *wants* to be."

"I'd say it depends on what she *has* to be. I have to be mature. I've got a boy to raise."

Jody was approaching the table, forestalling Dayt's reply. But as the three left the restaurant, his guiding hand rested lightly on the small of Gypsy's back, as if giving support for her task.

At the truck, Jody inexplicably decided he wanted to sit by the window, so Gypsy climbed in to ride in tantalizing nearness to Mr. Dayton O'Rourke, neighbor, business partner, and disturber of her volatile nature.

No one talked much on the way home; they were content to bask in the warm afterglow of a good meal and pleasant companionship. Dayt's arm, in a typically masculine gesture, rested behind Gypsy's head on the back of the seat. Every time she moved her head, she was aware of the soft brush of her hair against him. She tried to sit very still. Before long the mesmerizing sameness of the highway took its toll. Her eyes closed; her head nodded. She was asleep.

A jiggle. A soft murmur, "Gypsy? We're home." Rough tweed against the face.

She shot bolt upright, embarrassed to have fallen asleep like a baby on Dayt's shoulder. "Did—did I snore?"

"Like a freight train. Didn't she, Jode?" Both of the culprits started to laugh. "Not really, Gyps. Come on, let's get you into your beddy-bye." Dayt helped her out of the truck.

Once inside the house, Jody thanked Dayt for the evening and took off for his room with unexpected swiftness. No doubt he thinks we're going to kiss, or something, Gypsy mused. Little does he know.

The room was dimly lit from the one small lamp Gypsy had turned on upon their entrance. Dayt's face was shadowed, unreadable. He lounged in the doorframe without saying a word.

Gypsy, nervous, said, "Well, I don't want to keep a hard-working farmer out any later than necessary, so I won't offer to make coffee."

She half hoped he'd say, "Go ahead, make it," but he didn't. In her three-inch heels, she found herself looking directly into the strong column of his neck, wondering how many women had clung there, kissing him, inviting him without words to stay the night. She cleared her throat and said briskly, "Well, good night, Dayton."

A low, soft chuckle was his reply. He loomed over her, warm, dangerously tempting, and all the more desirable because he made no attempt to embrace her. His hand reached to cup her chin, and he gazed long into her unflinching violet eyes. She blushed as the memory of his hard, seeking kiss came back with devastating force. I don't want him to kiss me! she panicked. I don't want to be hurt again!

He laughed softly and dropped his hand. She stepped back out of range of his distracting charm. "Th—thank you, Dayt, for a lovely evening. And for the use of your shoulder," she added, trying to regain her composure with a little joke.

"You're more than welcome, Gyps. I must say, when I think of your sleeping with me, that's not quite what I have in mind."

She snapped at him without a moment's hesitation. "Don't! Don't think about me sleeping with you! We're strictly business, remember?"

He laughed. "Just joking. Don't worry, Gyps; the last thing I need in my life right now is a romantic entanglement with you. 'Night, Spitfire." He let himself out the door.

The call came at midnight. Gramps was dead.

Gypsy moved through the next few days in a state of frozen pain. How could it be? How could Gramps be improving daily, then suddenly, irretrievably, be gone? Her numbed mind revolved the questions endlessly, but no answer came.

It took two days to get a call through to Gypsy's parents at their remote New Guinea outpost. Their voices came thin and crackly over the line as Gypsy told them Gramps's express wish: that they not spend any of their meager resources to come home at this time. Their regular furlough was still a year off; it would take all they could round up to make that trip.

Gypsy loved her parents, yet they didn't seem quite real to her. Reality was lying cold and still at the funeral parlor.

Nevertheless, there were important chores to be done. The house must be readied; the stream of food from friends and neighbors properly stored for the funeral lunch; a record must be kept of every gift of food, flowers, or visitation so that prompt acknowledgement could be made. There was no end of work to keep Gypsy occupied during those days.

And then she and Jody, surrounded by Uncle Worth's family, were sitting in the plain little wooden church of her ancestors, listening to the biblical injunction that Christ is "the resurrection and the life." But Gypsy's ears were deaf to it. She concentrated on a patch of chipped ceiling paint, wondering how much it would cost to repair it. Through all these past days she hadn't cried, not once. It was as if the source of her feelings had dried to dust, left her a robot responding with automaton courtesy to the condolences proffered on every side.

Now they were at the graveyard. A warm, first-of-May breeze soughed through the pine boughs overhead. In accordance with Gramps's wishes for the simplest of ceremonies, there was no tent over his grave, and the family stood hand-in-hand, a human chain around the burial pit. The casket was lowered gently into its place, and Pastor James spoke clear words of Christian reassurance to the family and dozens who had come to see their old friend

Jesse off for his heavenly home. There were murmured amens. It was time for Gypsy to sing.

She'd never considered herself a singer, although Gramps had liked her true, full voice. She took a deep breath, and her eyes closed to the scene around her. The first notes were tentative, and then all of a sudden all the anguish, all her loneliness poured from her soul, lifted her voice in the Appalachian wail of "Take My Hand, Precious Lord" that was totally unlike any singing she'd ever done before. Some of the mourners looked around, unnerved by the raw grief in her tone. She didn't think about it; it simply welled from the depths of her stricken heart. But still the tears were denied.

The song was over. Gypsy stood, eyes still closed, until each of the other Connors had dropped one handful of dirt into the grave, then she threw in a single branch of forsythia from the backdoor bush at home, a tiny token of the sunshine Gramps had been in her life.

Aunt May and Uncle Worth had offered to have the after-funeral lunch at their home, but Gypsy insisted that Gramps's final party be in his own home. By the time the family got there, Aunt May's church circle was in full charge, the dining table loaded with sliced ham and beef, cold salads, hot casseroles, and the buffet supporting fifty-cup urns of coffee, iced tea, and lemonade. Guests began to arrive by the carload; naturally everyone who'd attended the funeral was expected to join the family afterward; it was ingrained Sauk Valley custom.

Gypsy went through the motions of hostessing, introducing Jody to those who didn't know him, trying with all her might to get back to "normal," to feel something other than the great lump sitting stonelike in her heart.

Dayt had stayed over for the funeral, of course, and he stood at some distance from her, talking to Tom and Uncle Worth but keeping his eyes on Gypsy. It was unusually warm for May, and Dayt, like most of the other men, had discarded the vest, tie, and jacket to his perfectly tailored gray linen suit. He looks like an ad for some swank man's product—shaving lotion or an expensive car—Gypsy reflected dispassionately.

"Gypsy, dear." Aunt May was by her side, a male distant cousin in tow. "Ned was wondering if Dad Connor had any old picture albums that you know of, something that might show the two of them together when they were little?"

"We played together all the time," Ned explained, fond reminiscence hovering in his elderly eyes. "It would mean a lot to me if I could have a picture of Jesse and me from then."

Gypsy's benumbed thoughts moved in slow motion to focus on the request. "Why—I think there might be something upstairs. I think Grandma kept a lot of those things packed away in boxes. I'll go see."

"Oh, I don't want to put you to all that bother," Cousin Ned protested.

"It's no trouble at all," Gypsy assured him, and slipped through the clots of people between her and the stairs to the second floor, glad to escape to even momentary solitude.

The low-ceilinged upper story was unneeded for bedroom space, so it had become a handy repository for just about everything under the sun. Gypsy had straightened it up and vacuumed out ten years' accumulation of dust when she and Aunt May did the housecleaning.

"Now, where did I see some old albums?" she murmured to herself, looking around at stacked cardboard boxes and sheet-covered relics of bygone days. She checked into various boxes; no luck. Her eyes caught on a battered trunk heaped with the carefully washed curtains she'd replaced downstairs. "I think it was in that trunk," she muttered. She set the curtains on the floor and opened the lid. The top layer was Gramps's Navy Seabee uniforms from World War II. She set them aside and continued digging. Just as she connected with the hard cover of an old-fashioned snapshot album, a doll leg popped out from under one of Grandma's crocheted tablecloths. Why, that must be—a tug revealed the whole doll—it was! Chatty Cathy, the best-loved doll of Gypsy's youth! Gypsy drew the pink-pajamaed baby doll from its longtime nest and sank back slowly on the pile of curtains. Chatty Cathy. Once she'd been the doll all little girls begged from Santa, as had Gypsy. She had a cord in her back that, when pulled, activated barely perceptible messages such as, "Hi! My name is Chatty Cathy. What's yours?"

Gypsy pulled the cord. Nothing happened. Poor old Cathy! She'd chatted her last long ago.

A sensation began to grow in the pit of Gypsy's stomach, an upheaval of emotion that had lain frozen for days. She remembered, vividly, the way Chatty had come into her six-year-old life: Grandma had turned a wicker clothes basket into a baby bassinet, telling Gypsy it was for the little Mears girl down the road. On Christmas Eve it had sat before the fireplace, supposedly awaiting delivery to the Mears household. While Gypsy and Grandma curled cozily in the big recliner reading "The Night Before Christmas," all the lights had mysteriously blinked out. There was a rustle at the fireplace, then the lights were restored by a straight-faced Gramps. In the bassinet lay Chatty Cathy with a note from Santa consigning her to the care of Miss Gypsy Connor. What joy had rung in Gypsy's heart! Never mind that other kids might have got three times as many presents as she; she'd got hers special delivered before Santa even started his run!

The love, the imagination that had gone into that short, caring charade swept Gypsy now, chased by the desolate knowledge that she would never again be anyone's "little girl." It astounded her to realize that she, who had been on her own for years, now felt for the first time the full emotional weight of being virtually parentless. She clutched the doll to her bosom, and her whole body convulsed around it as hot, salty tears coursed down her cheeks. Sobs contorted her, wracked her with their vehemence.

Vaguely she heard footsteps coming up the stairs. She recognized the tread, but she could do nothing to hide her agony from Dayt. Out of the corner of her eye she saw his sharp-creased pant leg within inches of her hunched figure.

"Gypsy?" He knelt, then sat beside her on the pile of curtains. She felt herself being gathered, babylike, into arms strong and tender. He cradled her head to his chest, and the crisp cleanness of his white shirt was immediately drenched. His hand moved gently to brush back the dark tendrils of hair matted to her face, and his head bent over hers as if he would protect her with every ounce of his being.

"There, there, little Gypsy girl," he crooned, swaying her

constricted body in a comforting rocking motion. "There, there. Cry it all out, sweet baby. You've got a right to cry."

His whispered words seemed to release new springs, and she wept with the need to empty herself of sorrow. He continued to hold her, to whisper meaningless little sounds of endearment, massaging carefully the back that ached from days of tension, until at last she was able to draw a shuddery breath and lie exhausted against his protective chest. He reached around to his back pocket to find a handkerchief to mop gently over her face.

"Dayt, I'm . . . I'm sorry—" Her half-choked whisper broke off.

"Sorry for what? For feeling everything, good or bad, so deeply? You won't be Gypsy any more when you don't do that." ·

Instinctively, she turned her face up to his, seeking blindly for warmth and understanding. The velvet of his lips pressed gently against her temples, her cheek, and then her mouth. Her right hand let go of the tight-clenched doll and clung to his neck, holding the life-line of his consolation until the thought that she was pushing herself onto him caused her to pull back, embarrassed.

"Oh . . . I didn't mean to start a kissing thing," she murmured.

"Shh-shh, it's just the grief, honey, just the grief. You need help with it, that's all," he soothed.

He understood. When had it ever meant more to her to be understood? She looked down at the doll's head exposed on her bosom. "I . . . suppose you must think I'm pretty silly, sitting here clutching a baby doll," she mumbled, "but it was a Christmas present, a very special one, from Gram and Gramps. Finding it just . . . threw me off balance."

His strong, hardened fingers stroked her hair back from her forehead, then paused to shelter her cheek and turn her face up to his. "I don't think there's anything silly about trying to keep love. I think it's the most natural thing in the world." He nestled the doll close to her breast, then wrapped his arms around her, much as a man protecting his wife and child.

"Oh, Dayt," she whimpered, "I miss Gramps so! I try to say he's with God, but I feel so . . . so cut off. Why does there have to be hurt like this?"

"I don't know," Dayt answered slowly. "I don't pretend to understand all about living or dying."

"I had so many easy assurances for Jody when his mother died. I said she'd gone to a better place. I said he'd be with her again some day. Now I feel like that was so shallow."

Dayt's arms tightened around her and his soft, deep voice vibrated her cheek where it lay pressed into his neck. "Gyps, honey, is that why you've cut Jody out of things the past three days?"

"Cut him out?" Gypsy pulled back to look up at Dayt, puzzled. "Is that what he thinks I've done?"

"He says you've been acting funny—that's the way he puts it—not talking to him, or even sitting down to the table with him since Jesse died. He's really worried about you, Gyps."

Gypsy dropped her head to his shoulder, ashamed of her inconsideration for Jody. "I haven't meant it that way. It's just that—well, how could I tell him how I feel? Ever since his mother died, I've been trying to show him that Christians have a special source of help. How can I tell him I'm not sure I believe that now that I'm the one who's suffering?"

87

Dayt lifted her face to his with gentle fingers. She searched his compassionate eyes for an answer.

"Can you honestly say that all the love, all the influence of your grandparents is gone now that they're gone?"

"Why, no, of course not," she responded slowly. "How could it be when it's built right into me?"

"Then maybe you shouldn't talk to Jody about what you doubt. Maybe you should tell him what you know, that love doesn't die with the human body. Which is stronger—what you doubt or what you know?"

She sat quietly a long time, eyes fastened to his, weighing the intelligence of his reply. At last she spoke, her voice a tremulous whisper. "Dayt, do you believe in God?"

He didn't answer with some immediate, trite assurance. Instead, he gazed down into the violet bruises that were her tear-smudged eyes. "Yes, I do, Gypsy," he answered at last. "And I believe that nothing dies. Oh, it changes form; you're aware of that, growing up on a farm; but nothing leaves this universe."

"Well—nothing *physical* leaves," she wavered.

"What's the realest part of a human, honey? A body? A body can be changed by accident or illness, and yet the reality of the person is still there. It's the soul that's the essence of a person, isn't it? If it's not real, then what is? I don't believe it just blinks out and is gone forever."

"Gramps . . . Gramps didn't believe that, either. He said we'd all be together, our whole family, one way or another, forever. I'll try, really hard, to remember that."

Dayt smiled down at her with an honest caring that would live in her memory always. "Don't force yourself, honey, just keep love, what you feel for your grandparents, what others feel for you. Nobody has come up with a better way to meet life than 'Love one another,' little Gypsy."

A consolation, slow and healing, began at that moment in Gypsy. Things that had seemed overwhelming started to fall back into perspective, and she felt relieved just to feel concern for Jody's welfare. Worry was far better than that horrible deadness of spirit that had weighted her the last three days.

"Thank you, Dayt," she said and lifted herself to kiss very gently his firm jaw, confident that he wouldn't misinterpret her motive. For some time she rested quietly in Dayt's strong sheltering. When she smelled fragrant coffee, ham, and warm rolls, hunger pangs, the first in days, began to stir.

"Come on, Dayt, let's go down and find Jody and have something to eat. He must feel awfully out of place down there with all those strangers."

Dayt helped her to her feet. "I'll bet he does," he agreed, giving her his arm and guiding her down the steep stairs. "From what he tells me, this whole farm and family experience is something of a cultural shock for him. But a good one."

Gypsy leaned on Dayt's supportive arm and marveled that she dared to like Dayton O'Rourke, as a person, as a Christian. Out of pain, maybe something good?

chapter

5

"I'LL DROP OFF THESE BOXES at the Salvation Army when I go into Shawana tomorrow," Aunt May offered. She, Gypsy, and Sheila had just finished sorting and packing Gramps's clothes and personal articles. "If you're sure you don't mind, I know Worth would love to have Dad's philosophy and theology collection. The two of them used to discuss St. Augustine and Calvin and Emerson—all those deep philosophers—by the hour."

"I don't mind, Aunt May," Gypsy said, taking one last look around the room once filled with Gramps's presence. "I tried working through some of those books to please Gramps, but frankly, they were above my head."

"You know what Pastor James says, 'Taking a plate of chocolate chip cookies to someone who's unhappy may be better Christianity than all the theology ever formulated.' And he's got a degree in the subject!"

"Speaking of cookies, let's take a tea break and dive into those oatmeal-everythings you brought over, Mom," Sheila suggested, leading the way out of Gramps's room, a big cardboard carton in her arms. Sheila was a vivacious blonde, tall, and what a catty woman might call "well-rounded." It was hard for Gypsy to believe how much she'd developed since she was a shy girl of thirteen.

"I'll make tea. What's an 'oatmeal-everything'?" Gypsy inquired on her way to the kitchen.

Sheila set down the carton to follow Gypsy. "Oh, you know Mom. She can't stick to a recipe for the life of her, so when she makes oatmeal cookies, she just throws in everything but the kitchen sink! Here, try one." She opened a Tupperware container sitting on the counter and offered Gypsy first chance at the toothsome rounds within.

"Ummm! If this is the result of ignoring a recipe, more power to her!" Gypsy mumbled, hand cupped under her chin to catch a falling bit of coconut.

Sheila took a cookie, nibbled at it, and laughed. "Mom's a great old girl, isn't she, Gyps? But old-fashioned." Her voice lowered significantly. "I can't tell you how glad I am to have some female family around that I can *talk* to. Sometimes I feel like Mom and I are in two different worlds."

"How so?" Gypsy had always found Aunt May wonderfully easy to communicate with. When Grandma died, Aunt May had taken Gypsy to her heart with all the tenderness of a blood mother.

Sheila leaned against the counter to elaborate. "Do you know what she says—openly says—she wishes for you and me? That we marry two nice Sauk Valley men and settle down right here to raise her some grandbabies!"

"And you don't like that idea?" Gypsy smiled, amused.

"That's not the point, Gyps. How many handsome, well-to-do, available men do you think there are in this place? I can think of one—Dayton O'Rourke. He's the greatest hunk in six counties! But I've never known him to even go out with a local girl, let alone propose."

Dayt's name caught Gypsy off-guard; she busied herself getting out tea things, avoiding Sheila's eyes. Any mention of Dayt stirred the strange new feeling of respect mixed with a possessiveness toward him that had grown in her heart since the day of the funeral. It bothered her to hear him referred to as a mere "hunk"; he had proved to her how much more he was than some mindless macho man depending upon rippling muscles to establish his masculinity.

"There's a lot to be considered besides a man's wealth or looks, She-She," she counseled. "Dayt would be special even if he were homely and poor."

"Mmm. Maybe so." Sheila shrugged. "But you've got to admit, his money and looks don't exactly make him dogmeat! Anyhow," she continued over Gypsy's assenting laughter, "I'm going to look into something a little more exciting than my bank job, because, as I tell Mom, a career may turn out to be a lot easier to come by than a husband. Which reminds me, what are you going to do now, Gyps? Go back on the road?"

"I really don't know, Sheila." Gypsy had asked herself the same question about a thousand times in the past week. She'd made the rounds of every possible employer within a twenty-mile radius, so far to no avail. There was something she'd considered, but she wasn't sure if she could handle it.

The shrill of the teakettle pierced the tête-à-tête and brought Aunt May out to the kitchen. Over a refreshing cup of spiced oolong, she asked fretfully, "Did I hear you girls mention Dayt's name?"

"Oh, slightly," Sheila replied, tossing Gypsy a knowing wink. "Why?"

"It's that boarding-house thing. I just don't know what I'm going to do about housing that acting company! Everyone I've approached has found one reason or another why they can't take them in. You know," she went on after a delicate bite of cookie, "the men stayed at Dayt's house last weekend while they were working on the barn. I met Reva Thompson in the grocery Monday, and she carried on just something awful about all the work it made for her, cooking for them and cleaning up after them and all. If she keeps telling that around, I'll never get anyone to take the whole group." She sipped her tea. "I don't like to say it, but really, Reva is just an awfully fussy person. I don't see how Mike Thompson has put up with her persnickety ways all these years." Aunt May looked around guiltily, immediately sorry for her uncharacteristic belittling of another.

"Fussy? Sour is more like it, Mom," Sheila averred. "I happen to know Dayt pays her plenty for every lick of extra work she does—I've cashed some of her checks from him—and she has the nerve to go around complaining like she was some kind of serf."

"Well, of course, she *does* have a lot to do, taking care of two houses," Aunt May excused, already trying to see the irascible Reva in the best possible light. "At any rate, I've got to come up with something by Saturday. I understand the whole company is coming down then for the season."

"There's a lot to do before the barn is ready," Gypsy said. "They carted out about three tons of dust and junk, but they've still got to build the stage, put in the lights and restroom, and all that." Her heart did a little skip; Dayt would be here Friday. That interested her more than what was going on out at the barn.

"When's the first performance? The first weekend in June? It's already the tenth of May," Sheila put in. "Think they'll be ready?"

"If I know show-biz types, they'll open on schedule if they have to work around the clock," Gypsy stated. She went to the stove to refill the teapot with hot water. "You know. . ." She hesitated, then came forth with the idea she'd been mulling for the past two days. "I've been thinking. Why couldn't the acting company live here? I know," she hurried on at Aunt May's doubting glance, "we're short of bedrooms, but—" She set down the teapot to launch better into her proposal. "If I took Gramps's room, and Jody slept on the office day bed, the girls and Ila could take our two rooms, and the guys could bunk upstairs. It's not fancy, but it would be handy to their work, and I could get some cheap wallpaper and stuff and make things reasonably attractive. What do you think, Aunt May?"

"Oh. . . well—"

"Neat! That's a great idea, Gyps!" Sheila burst out. "I'll help you nights after work. I'm bored stiff with sitting home listening to a phone that doesn't ring!"

"Well, Gypsy honey, you'd be taking on quite a job. There'd be meals, and laundry, and other things like that. And the apprentices; don't forget they have to have supper on performance nights." Aunt May paused, apparently wavering between relief at having a big problem solved and lack of confidence in Gypsy's qualifications for the role of "housemother."

"I know, Aunt May. But let's face it: I could use the income and I'm probably the only person around here who understands the somewhat erratic schedule of entertainers."

"That's very true, dear." Aunt May chewed her lower lip over the decision. "As to the cooking, I could help you with that. If there's one thing I know about, it's meal planning for a hungry crew! But Dayton. What would he say about it? He may worry about your . . . uh . . . lack of experience?"

Aunt May's discreet reminder that Gypsy had done very little home managing was wasted. "Dayt's not got much choice, has he? It's either that or turn them loose in his beautiful home, minus the service of Reva. I don't think he's going to opt for that. We'll just present him with the accomplished fact when he shows up Friday." Besides the reasons she'd given Aunt May for taking in the boarders, she had a deep desire to please Dayt by helping him out of a sticky situation. It was important to her, more so every day, to win his approval, to have him think of her as a friend who could give as well as take. "Come on, Aunt May, She-She, let's go upstairs and start packing all the boxes and trunks into the back room. I think I can figure out a way to get three single beds into the main room. . . ."

The three climbed the stairs to the accompaniment of Gypsy's and Sheila's enthusiastic plans to turn the upper story into a veritable bachelor haven. It was so good to have a big project to work on, something to absorb her energies and keep her mind off her recent bereavement, Gypsy explained to that tiny corner of her mind that kept saying, Are you sure you're ready for this? Once again impulse was the driving force behind her actions.

*   *   *

"Oh. . . my . . . goodness!" The words dropped like three separate leaden weights from Gypsy's anguished lips.

Her dirge was barely heard over Dayt's deep-rumbled, "What on earth *is* this mess?"

"But it was all right when I left five minutes ago to let you in! What . . . why . . . ?"

They stood in the middle of the big room; over their heads strips of wallpaper applied over a four-hour period dangled limply.

"I don't understand. I followed the store manager's directions to the letter! Why is it all falling off?" Gypsy struggled to keep her voice below hysteria level. She was exhausted; her arms ached unbearably; it was clear she and Sheila would have to work all night to get the side walls done; but worst of all, Dayt was staring at her as if she were a crazy woman.

"What *I* don't understand is whatever made you think you could hang wallpaper? Especially this old-fashioned kind that has to be pasted. Couldn't you at least have got that prepasted stuff you just dip in water?"

"It costs too much," Gypsy defended. "I got this on sale."

"A real savings," Dayt stated dryly, reaching up to catch a strip of the beige ceiling paper before it fell on Gypsy's head. "Gypsy, this is just like the rest of your scheme—preposterous. You have no more business trying to run a boarding house for actors than you have trying to play paperhanger. The whole thing is going to be a disaster from the word 'go.'"

"It is not! I'll . . . I'll figure out a way to make this paper

96

stick if I have to staple it up!" Gypsy vowed. "And the side walls—just look how handsome this paper is!" she insisted, grabbing a roll of as yet unapplied accent paper to display its black, beige, and white plaid. "This is for the west wall. Isn't it stunning?"

"Marvelous. Use it to wrap presents," Dayt snorted. He took her by the shoulders and forced her to meet his severe gaze. "Gypsy, honey, the paper is just the beginning. Do you have any idea what kind of responsibility you're taking on? You'll be tied down night and day. You've never in your life had to take care of more than two people at a time. Think of all the meals, the laundry—"

Aunt May had guessed right. Well, Dayt was about to learn that Gypsy Connor, eager though she was to please him, friend though she now considered him, was still her own boss.

"I've made up my mind, Dayt. It's my house and my life. I'm going to set down rules and assign jobs to everyone so that I don't have to do all the work. And Aunt May is going to give me her expert advice on budget meals for a large group. You *know* how good her food is."

"Granted. But I have a feeling there's a small difference between planning those meals and actually getting them on the table three times a day. You can't feed them hot dogs and marshmallows for *every* meal."

That snide remark snapped Gypsy's tired shoulders to full attention. "Now Dayton O'Rourke, just get that bulldog lawyer look off your face and stop talking silly! Of course I can't feed them hot dogs and marshmallows! You might as well accept the inevitable: your business partner has made a decision and she's going to stick with it!"

Dayt's exasperated air gradually lightened, and he allowed a wry grin. "*I'm* a bulldog? I told you, Gypsy, you aren't going to get your way with me like you did with Jesse. It'll be ninety days before you come into the money Jesse saved for you and until then, I control the purse strings, remember? What if I won't agree to financing this undertaking?"

Gypsy's smile was slow and guileless. "A few weeks ago words like that would have made me see red. But I haven't forgotten what happened in this room the day of Gramps's funeral. You helped me so much, Dayt." She put a pleading hand on his arm. "And I'm counting on your understanding now. Remember what you said about men paying their own way? Well, don't you think a woman could have the same pride?"

Dayt's warm hand covered hers, and the stubbornness seeped out of his bearing. Still, he wasn't convinced. "Gypsy, honey," he said gently, "I'm not putting down your need to feel independent, but can't you fulfill it some other way? Can't you find some easier job to tide you over till the estate's settled? Or if it'll make you feel better, I'll loan you money against your share of the farm. If you can't repay it, I'll take enough land to satisfy the note and we'll be even."

She pulled away from him, adamant. "No, Dayt. You've already loaned me enough cash for my miscellaneous expenses. And I won't sign away any land as long as there's any possible way to avoid it. Oh, I know," she hastened to assure him, "you're not trying to weasel it away from me. It's just . . . I've lost so much already; somehow, the land is a connection, a visible reminder of what . . . who I came from." Her troubled eyes clung to his. "Does that make any sense?"

Dayt nodded a slow agreement, compassion softening his eyes. "But can't you even try for some other work that would support you and Jody for the next few months?"

She moved away to wad up a strip of wallpaper lying messily paste-side-down on the floor. "I've checked in Sauk Valley and Shawana; there's nothing, not even a store clerk's job, open right now. If I go farther away from home, I'll be leaving Jody more or less on his own for hours every day, and that's the last thing he needs. Sure, the acting company will be around here, but they're going to be wrapped up in their own concerns; they won't have time to play counselor to a needy teenager. I took him to raise. It's my responsibility to give him more than food and shelter, isn't it?"

Dayt shook his head resignedly, then chuckled. "Gyps, you should be a lawyer. You could wear down the toughest opponent! Well . . ." He turned, fists on hips, to survey the stricken room. "If you're bound to go through with this, I guess there's nothing to do but help you." He looked at his watch. "It's two o'clock Friday; the gang will be here by noon tomorrow. I'd say our first order of business is to tear off all this gunk, then go into town and get some paint. That'll go on those slanting walls a lot easier than paper."

"But the cracks? I thought paper would hide the cracks and blemishes better?"

"Forget it, Toots. We'll have all we can do to get a coat of paint on and the furniture moved in. You *have* got beds, haven't you? You're not planning to make them out of orange crates or something?" He started yanking off

Gypsy's painstakingly applied wallpaper while she gathered it for disposal.

"Yes, Mr. Smart, I have beds!" she shot back saucily. "I've begged, borrowed, and almost stolen from all our neighbors. I've got a set of bunk beds to put along the end wall, and a single to tuck in under this slanting one. Downstairs I've got two singles in my old room and two in what was Jody's. He'll sleep on the daybed in Gramps's office."

"What about your grandfather's room? Is that for Ila?"

"No." Gypsy straightened, arms loaded with paper. "That'll be my room." The idea of a stranger in Gramps's room—it was unthinkable.

Dayt's arms lowered before he pulled off the last strip of paper. "You expect Ila to share a room with one of the girls?" His gaze was incredulous.

"Well . . . yes. You expect *me* to share a room with a stranger? It's my house."

"And it's your responsibility to provide Ila with a decent room of her own. She's no kid, you know. She'll need privacy."

"Well . . . well . . . , " Gypsy began to splutter, "I'm no kid, either. And why should I let some utter stranger have Gramps's room?"

"Because it's exactly what your grandfather would have done. Can you imagine Jesse expecting a mature lady like Dr. Danova to 'bunk in' with someone else?" He shook his head. "This is why I have my doubts. You're not going to be the star of this show, Gypsy. For once in your life, you're going to be in the background while someone else takes center stage."

"Blast it!" she blared out with her old-time fieriness, "if you're so concerned about Dr. Danova's comfort, why don't you let her live at your house?"

"Ila does not 'live with' men. Do you think you're the only woman with scruples against that sort of thing?"

He had her there. First, he'd used Jesse against her, now her own standards. She stood in snappy-eyed wrath for a second, then it passed as quickly as it had come.

"Okay," she consented mildly, "Ila the Queen shall have Gramps's room. I'll even start her day with a polite tap at her door and a pot of exclusive coffee, if you think her artistic temperament needs it," she joked good-naturedly.

Dayt laughed. "Don't get smart, Missy, or my unartistic temperament may turn you over my knee!"

"Ha! Don't you wish?" she teased. "I'll tell you one thing for sure, Dayton O'Rourke: if these people, Ila included, are really professional in their attitude, they'll sleep on a bed of nails and eat grass for a chance to perform before the public. *That's* the spirit of true entertainers."

Dayt's mouth screwed into a tongue-in-cheek grin. "I defer to your expert knowledge, O Hotheaded One. Lead me to the trash pile."

Arms piled high with the spoiled fruits of Gypsy's morning labor, the two of them descended to the first floor.

"*'Another* fine mess you've got us into, Stanley!' " Dayt flashed her an Oliver Hardy grin.

Gypsy stood at the open front door and gazed across the porch to the van sitting in the driveway. Behind her was a house cleaned within an inch of its life and scented everywhere with the fragrance of fresh lilacs and apple blossoms. Upstairs was a dormitory room newly painted, thanks to Dayt, in off-white with deep tan trim to match the striped black, white, and tan sheets fitted snuggly over the beds and gracing the dormer windows in the form of short drapes. Down the hall off the living room three bedrooms stood ready to serve the female inhabitants of her home, suitably done up with flowered sheets and pastel curtains. Gypsy had taken special pains with Gramps's old room. After the chagrin at having to give it up to Ila had died down, she'd determined to make the older woman as comfortable as possible, with a rocking chair and a tiny corner table and seat where she could, indeed, have a private cup of coffee or a meal if she so desired. Gypsy envisioned her as a middle-aged professional type who'd need more time and space to recharge her batteries than the under-thirty crowd living around her.

Shock number one was about to hit Gypsy. She, with Aunt May on one side and Sheila on the other, watched as Dayt, Jody right behind him, strode to the van and opened the front passenger door. Other doors were already opening, ejecting three pretty jean-clad girls and the same number of healthy-looking young men. Gypsy had met the men the weekend before, and they seemed like nice enough sorts.

Now Dayt lifted a hand to aid the descent of his "old high school teacher" from the van. Gypsy took one look and nearly yelped with surprise. Alighting, face aglow with smiling acceptance of Dayt's helpfulness, was a stunning auburn-haired beauty standing nearly as tall as Dayt in her high-heeled slides. A pure white cotton jumpsuit outlined her firm, sensuously curved figure, and she lifted one hand to smooth her thick, shoulder-length tresses with the graceful gesture of a woman sure of her own glamour. All the while her heavy-lidded green eyes rested in undisguised affection on Dayt's equally appreciative face.

A cold pang of envy ripped through Gypsy. *This* was the woman of whom he'd been so solicitous? If Ila was a day over thirty-eight, you couldn't tell it from here, Gypsy moaned inwardly.

"Wow! Is *that* Dr. Danova?" Sheila whispered, just as awe-struck as her cousin.

"What an . . . attractive . . . woman," murmured Aunt May, clearly doing some revamping of her expectations. "She doesn't look much like our Mrs. Wilks, does she?" she continued, mentioning the pleasant, plump, over-fifty English teacher who presided over Sauk Valley High's theatrical efforts.

Gypsy resolutely shoved aside her jealous twinges and stepped onto the porch. Ila's appearance was no more shocking to her than the instant's realization that she, Gypsy, had in the past ten days come to think of Dayt as her special friend, so special that it hurt, terribly, to see him falling all over Dr. Danova.

No, Gypsy corrected herself as she opened the screen door and fastened a welcoming smile on her face, it wasn't right to say Dayt was falling all over Ila. He was greeting her with a warm, admiring respect he'd never turned on Gypsy, but was that Ila's fault? Or his?

Now the entourage was moving toward the porch steps, Jody leading the way like a proud young host. How much more maturely he's behaving since we came here, mused Gypsy. Since he's known Dayt.

"Ila," Dayt said, handing her up the steps to meet her hostess, "may I introduce my friend, neighbor, and business partner, Mary Catherine Connor, otherwise known as 'Gypsy.'"

Gypsy broadened her smile and held out her hand to the glorious woman who returned her smile and met her open gaze with one equally frank. There was friendship in Ila's aspect, but also steel. Her handshake was brief but surprisingly firm, considering the softness of her impeccably manicured fingers, one of which, the left hand ring finger, bore a gold band studded with emeralds fiery and cold at the same time.

" 'Mary Catherine'? What a beautiful name! And 'Gypsy'? I like that even better!" Ila's deep green eyes lightened with a sunny sparkle that disarmed Gypsy, at least for the moment.

"Dr. Danova, I've looked forward to meeting you. Please come in, all of you," Gypsy urged, looking from Ila's mesmerizing face to the others waiting at the base of the stairs. "I'll take you on a tour of the premises and then we'll have lunch," Gypsy promised, leading the way into the dining room where the table was set for an Aunt-May-inspired feast of fried chicken and potato salad.

A flurry of introductions followed, after which Gypsy added the names of Theresa Shores, Sandra Weber, and Jo Ann Sparks to her list of acquaintances. The men, Mark Tanner, Shawn Richards, and Daniel Wells, introduced themselves to Aunt May and Sheila, who took in their youthful good looks with a pleased eye. Later, Gypsy knew, Sheila would have plenty to say about Mark's dark handsomeness, the lithe power obvious in Shawn's tall frame, and the astonishingly rich highlights in Dan's tawny-gold hair.

As for the girls, dark-haired Theresa was tall and large boned, pretty in her big-is-beautiful way; Sandy was the all-American girl with brown hair and a peaches-and-cream complexion. Jo Ann Sparks lived up to her nickname "Sparky" every inch of the way. She was small and bright, a bundle of energy tanned dark in contrast to the white-blond fluff of hair haloing her animated face.

Amidst a rush of contradictory feelings, Gypsy led the group from the dining room, living room, and bedrooms, to the kitchen and up to the men's "dorm," then down to the basement laundry room. The old house had always seemed relatively large to her, but now, filled with six lively young boarders, an aunt, a cousin, a ward, Dayt, Ila, and herself, there didn't seem to be much room anywhere. All through the delicious lunch Aunt May had insisted upon preparing for this first day of Gypsy's new career as housemother, Gypsy had strange, fluttery disturbances in her middle. Looking around the oak table stretched to seat twelve, she experienced a tremendous fear that she'd bitten off more than she could chew. Had Dayt been right? *Was* she capable of feeding nine people three meals a day (plus twelve apprentices on performance nights), overseeing the endless chores of a big household, managing the money so that the modest fee she was charging her "guests" would cover expenses? One thing was certain: these were no pick-at-a-piece-of-lettuce dieters sitting at her table! All of them, including Ila, were putting away substantial quantities of Aunt May's good provender, openly relishing every bite.

Dayt sat at one end of the table, Aunt May at the other;

her chipmunky-cute face beamed with the compliments heaped on her cookery.

Oh, no! Gypsy panicked, what'll they think of *my* cooking? *Please, dear Lord, have mercy on me, an impulsive fool, and guide my hand every time it comes near the cook pot!*

When the meal finally concluded, Gypsy explained what to her were simple enough house rules. She would post a list of household duties such as table setting, dishwashing, and laundry on the kitchen door and they could sign up for weekly turns at each. She, of course, would be in charge of food purchasing and preparation (her throat clicked a little over that part) and the cleaning of the common rooms. Would they please remember that the water supply came from a well and try never to wash a less than full load of clothes, or to dawdle in the shower? And, oh, yes, the garden . . .

"Aunt May and Sheila have helped me plant a large garden, as I'm sure you'll all enjoy a plentiful supply of fresh vegetables, so I'll ask you to also sign up for turns at weeding and harvesting. I'll take the first two weeks while you're getting the barn ready to go and auditioning the day students, but I won't be able to handle it after that, so I'll appreciate your help."

Gypsy sat back in her chair, relieved to be delivered of her oration, and surreptitiously glanced at her watch. Only four more hours before she had to have a six o'clock supper on this table!

"If . . . if you'll excuse me now," she blurted, "I have to start my afternoon duties." She rose shakily, aware of Ila's amusedly assessing perusal and Dayt's doubting one, and headed for the kitchen. This was going to be one rough day!

The next two weeks passed in a blur. Hammering poured incessantly from the barn, underscoring the endless vocalizations of the auditioning hopefuls on the front porch, where Ila had set up shop. The girls, when not helping with construction in the barn, were finding or making costumes or props, and Gypsy learned the first law of theater: never buy anything you can make or borrow. Nothing was sacred from their predatory prowlings of the house and attic storage room. Did she mind if they used that small end table, the antique love seat, and the brass floor lamp for the first production?

No, of course not. They *would* use the love seat gently, wouldn't they? It was more than a hundred years old.

Oh, sure. Say, have you got any old material, drapes or something, we could make some long skirts out of? Doesn't have to be any particular color; we'll dye it to suit—oh, you don't care if we dye in your washing machine, do you?

On and on the requests and depredations came, and Gypsy couldn't make herself say no because she understood the imperative need to make do with what was at hand. But still, when she snatched a minute to look around her cannibalized living room, noticed the sewing machine set up on Grandma's walnut drop leaf table because there was no room for it elsewhere, saw the threads and scraps of material littering what had been a scrupulously neat room, it did bother her. It was funny because a year ago she'd had little interest in maintaining a more than passable tidiness in her housekeeping, but ever since she and Aunt May had worked so hard to brighten this home for Gramps's anticipated return—no use in grumbling. She understood. Time was short and the show must go on.

Dayt had ordered the parking lot white rocked, and it was a good thing because cars came and went constantly while the auditions were on. The thought of a lot full of mired cars some rainy day was more than Gypsy could face.

Dayt also had the plumbers install a shower for the men of the company off the public bathroom in the barn, taking a load off the sorely burdened bath-and-a-half at the house.

Gypsy met herself coming and going. If she wasn't preparing a meal, she was at the grocery loading up for one. "Half again," she told Aunt May at the beginning of the second week. "They consume half again what we thought they would. I thought maybe my cooking would slow them down, but apparently they've got strong stomachs!"

"Well, now, Jody and Dayt both say you're a pretty good chef. Dayt said you asked him to stay to Sunday brunch last week, and it was delicious."

"Oh . . . did he?" That's all it took, one word of praise from Dayt, to make her forget how tired she'd been last Sunday when she'd arisen at five to get everything ready for a festive brunch after ten o'clock church services. She hadn't heard a word of Pastor James's sermon; Dayt had come to sit next to her, driving out every thought except how good it was to have him beside her, how hopeful she was that he'd accept her invitation to brunch, especially since Ila had gone back to Chicago for the day. When Ila and Dayt were in the same room, they always seemed to end up in a secluded corner, talking over something that made their faces serious and brought out that protective look in Dayt's eyes that Gypsy wanted reserved for herself alone. The thought crossed her mind more than once:

108

could Ila be the woman Dayt had been "involved" with five years ago? And could they be patching up whatever it was that had split them apart? The possibility stirred not-so-pretty emotions in Gypsy, feelings she knew she should be talking over with God the way she used to. But now God sometimes seemed far away. It was Dayt to whom she looked for guidance, even though she might resist it at the moment he was giving it. Dayt was real. God seemed like just a name.

By the middle of the second week, Gypsy and Ila had had their first confrontation, a mild one, it was true, and won by Gypsy, but she had a hunch it wouldn't be the last time their wills collided. It was over the naming of the barn. Ila's troupe was called the New Earth Players and she wanted that name on the barn. Gypsy had gone along with almost every request from Ila and her company, but not this time.

"The name will be 'Jesse's Barn,'" she announced after a supper table mulling of the subject.

Ila had politely demurred, "But 'New Earth' symbolizes our very purpose to help bring in a new age when every life, every effort is Christ-centered. And at the same time, it ties in with a country setting for our theater."

"Yes, I see that," Gypsy had agreed, "but 'Jesse's Barn' is even more meaningful to me because not only was the biblical Jesse the 'root of our faith,' but my grandfather, Jesse Connor, was the truest Christian I ever knew. I want his spirit to preside over the barn he helped build and wanted dedicated to God's service. So it'll be 'Jesse's Barn.'"

"As you wish." Ila's acquiescence was gracious, but

nevertheless, it didn't cover a momentary flash in her emerald eyes. Apparently contradiction of her wishes was new to her.

Actually there was little time for anyone to stay angry over anything, as opening night, the first Friday in June, was upon them with lightning speed. For that event, Gypsy, Jody, and Dayt sat in the only unsold seats in the "house," just as gratified as were the players by the excellent turnout for the first production of the season. Most of the audience of a hundred and fifty or so were locals, drawn as much by curiosity as by any strong affinity with theater, but Ila had wisely chosen a lively musical comedy, a modern-day version of Noah's story designed to provoke laughter not at the Lord, but at the foibles of his children. It was part of the company's previous repertoire, so the newly chosen apprentices were relegated to ticket selling and stage crew while the experienced players, accompanied by Ila at the piano rented for the season, sang, danced, and cavorted, much to the audience's delight.

Jody had never seen live professional theater; he sat absorbed as the skillful players brought to vibrant life what had started as a few scratches of pen on paper. "They're really good, aren't they, Gypsy?" he enthused when the audience rose for a standing ovation after the finale. "Do you suppose they'd let me have a part? Just a small one?" he wondered. "I'd even like to work stage crew, just to see what goes on when they're practicin'."

"Well, it wouldn't hurt to ask Ila," Gypsy answered over the continuing applause. "Only remember, your first duty is to Dayt's lawn; you agreed to do it and you can't neglect it for a new love. Besides, you'll need the money."

"Thanks, Gyps! I'll ask Ila tonight while she's feelin' good about the opening. And I won't forget Dayt's lawn, I promise."

"You'd better not," Dayt warned from Jody's left side, "or I'll sic Reva on you. She can't stand a blade of grass more than an inch high!"

Dayt insisted on treating the cast and crew, plus Gypsy and Jody, to a party after the show, so at eleven-thirty the whole triumphant crowd spilled into his big dark brick and oak house for pizza and soft drinks supplied in plentiful quantities from Sauk Valley's only pizza parlor. Before anyone could sink a tooth into the mouth-watering *piece de resistance,* Dayt brought out a festive bowl of Reva's sparkly golden punch.

"May I propose a toast," he said, raising his glass, "to the newest addition to theater history, Jesse's Barn, and to the most accomplished combination of talent and beauty I know, Ila Danova!"

Jealousy stabbed to the very pit of Gypsy's heart. While others cheered and drank their toasts, she managed only to hold her face immobile and take one scant sip. *Help me, Lord,* she prayed. *I know he's right; I know Ila is everything I'm not—disciplined, well-educated, sophisticated—but does he have to say so? Help me to control this sinful envy.*

But though she prayed, the words seemed sealed from heaven by the picture of Dayt and Ila, touching glasses, smiling happily into each other's eyes.

After the punch, everyone fell to the scrumptious pizzas set forth in all their pungent glory on the oak buffet. Everyone but Gypsy. She was too sick with envy to be hungry; she wandered away from the noisy group pillaging the food and explored the house she hadn't entered for five years past. She didn't want to be a wet blanket on the festivities, so she roamed into the living room, seeing the plush silver-gray carpet, the massive contemporary furniture upholstered in shades of gray and off-white, spiked by artistic touches of vivid reds, yellows, and greens. She had always liked this rugged house that seemed to grow right out of the prairie, even though it was much different from the homey clutter of a Connor residence. It had a clean yet sophisticated strength that reminded her of Dayt himself.

She sat down at the big black Steinway. She knew what was wrong with herself, and she was ashamed of it. For the first time in her life, little Gypsy Connor and her musical skills and good looks weren't the center of Sauk Valley's attention—worse yet, of Dayton O'Rourke's attention. Someone far more accomplished was. *I'm learning the hard way,* she thought, *what it's like to be the background support system, the unspectacular serf who moils and toils that others may shine. And I don't like it!*

All night her hands had itched to beat out the swingy music of the play, especially to give it her own unique touch. Her fingers slid lightly onto the keys; of their own volition they picked out the melody of the opening number and then suddenly she knew, *knew* without thinking, how the thing should go. She hadn't touched a keyboard for two weeks, but now the love for it took over and she lost all her bitter feelings in the pure joy of producing happy music.

She didn't notice how the laughing chatter from the dining room had died down; she was oblivious to everything but her own pleasure until a sudden feeling of being watched shot through her and whirled her around on the bench.

"Oh!" Her breath caught sharply as she saw the wide living room entrance filled with the partiers. Applause and cries of "Keep going! You're really good!" broke out, and Ila came forward, her face a strange mixture of puzzlement and reluctant admiration.

"Gypsy! You didn't tell me you were a musician! You must have been practicing this on the sly. You're better than I am!"

"No, oh, no!" Gypsy faltered, disconcerted by the attention. "I just . . . hack around on the piano. I'm . . . no musician."

"But you are! False modesty isn't necessary." Ila sat down beside her. "Do you realize what this means? If you can play like that, I can be free to act, which is what I really love to do. Try that last song in the key of E flat, the one Sandy sings it in."

"E . . . flat? What note would that start on?" Gypsy had never in her life felt so illiterate of technical knowledge.

"You don't know one key signature from another?" Ila asked incredulously.

"No." Gypsy looked up at her, miserably uncomfortable. "I've never had to. I just play by ear, and since I've always worked solo—except for church services, of course—who cared what key I played in? I just picked out the easiest version." Deep red flooded up and over her face; she sounded like an ignoramus.

"Well, can you read notes?" Ila inquired, still staring at her.

"Oh, yes, I know that much." Gypsy felt Dayt's gaze on

her and wanted to fade into the woodwork. This was confirmation of his severest criticism of her musical skill; it was uninformed. Because she was lazy.

The others were all crowding around the piano waiting for Gypsy to play on, but still Ila prodded her. "I could teach you in one afternoon how to read key signatures and then you could transpose into whatever key was needed. It shouldn't be difficult for anyone with your natural feel for music. Will you help us? Join the company?"

Gypsy looked up at Dayt. Oh, how she longed to be part of the entertainment instead of the drudge behind the scenes. But could she manage it all?

"I think you could do it, Gyps," Dayt encouraged. "You'll never have a better teacher than Ila."

If he'd dropped a bucket of ice water on her he could have no more effectively chilled her. So this was to be one more chance for Ila to shine in his eyes?

"I . . . don't see how I can do it and still meet all my other obligations."

"I'll get someone to help with your housework," Dayt eagerly put forth.

"No! Perhaps . . . in an emergency—" Gypsy rose from the piano bench. Turning down this chance was the hardest thing she'd ever done in her career, but to put herself under the tutelage of Ila, to win Dayt's approval only because she, too, acknowledged Ila's superior talent? No. She couldn't do it.

"Oh. I . . . understand." Ila's cool answer showed she understood, all right; Gypsy was rebuffing her offer on personal grounds. Ila, too, stood. The whole party, subdued, drifted back to the dining room, but not before

Gypsy caught Dayt's stern-jawed glare right in the center of her sensitive heart.

chapter

6

IF THE PACE AT JESSE'S BARN was hectic before opening night, it was even faster afterward, because now, besides six performances a week, rehearsals, singing, dancing, and acting lessons had to be worked in. Then there were the writing sessions. Since the company wrote most of its material, hours were spent around the big oak table brainstorming, writing, revising. Gypsy, in spite of her jealousy of Ila, was fascinated by the way material evolved. While she worked around the house, she listened in on the lively creative sessions. Usually a theme was chosen first, a Christian principle to be delineated. Then came the plot. An idea, a "what if," would be thrown out, examined from various viewpoints, incorporated into a possible plot line. Until it had been kicked around for awhile, no one knew whether it would be handled humorously or seriously, or both as sometimes happened. The young men came up with the more original ideas, but the young women were better at fleshing them out with dialogue. Gypsy noticed Ila usually stayed in the background, only stepping in with some judicious editing or rearrangement. Plot ideas came from everywhere—the newspapers, television, local functions, but especially from the Bible. Never before had Gypsy realized what a storehouse of comic-tragic story lines that ancient bastion of wisdom was. Stories that stirred an uneasy question—

That the universe had to start with some superior being, that human nature remained unchanged from the days of Eden, she could see. But the guiding force behind this long-playing drama—*was* it a loving Father? Were we deluding ourselves to believe there was a source of comfort in this world other than what we could offer each other? Sometimes a terrible fear niggled at her mind: maybe God had left his creation to fend for itself. She tried to push the question away, afraid to press for an answer.

The company kept a loose schedule. Mornings began with private meditations until Gypsy opened the "breakfast bar" at eight. From then till noon everyone worked at individual writing, acting, or household projects. Gypsy served the main meal of the day at twelve and a sandwich-and-soup type supper at six. At one the apprentices arrived for rehearsals and lessons, except on Wednesday afternoons, which were kiddie matinees, and Sundays, which were days of rest. Supposedly. Once the Sauk Valley choir directors learned there was a group of professional Christian performers at hand, New Earth was invited to do the special music at one church or another every single Sunday morning! Sabbath evenings the group kept reserved for informal worship services in the barn to revitalize their energies and ask the Lord's inspiration for all that they would do in the coming week.

It was an ambitious schedule, but for a while things went fairly smoothly. Then holes appeared here and there in the fabric. Sometimes people were right in the middle of an important project when they were supposed to be doing a household chore. What were they to do? Jeopardize a production just to carry out the garbage or set the table? Gypsy understood their priorities; hadn't she had the same ones most of her life? But it did throw more and more burdens on her because Jody had wangled his way onto the stage crew for the present production, and between those duties and his yard work at Dayt's, Gypsy saw little of him.

And the weather tuned up. An Illinois summer is an unpredictable beast, Gypsy remembered. It can go from cold to rainy to hot and muggy with barely a pause for effect. Or, as in the case of the present summer, it could sustain a heat wave for weeks with unwavering tenacity. By the end of June, Gypsy had installed window fans all over her house, and still there were nights when sleep was impossible due to the stifling heat.

Of all the boarders, Ila was the least complaining. Day after day she went about, always looking fresh and fit in her shorts and knit tops, always wafting a scent of exotic flowers in her wake as she planned, directed, performed, taught, moving from one activity to the other with no difficulty at all. She did no household chores, but Gypsy could hardly fault her for that, since she seemed to be busy every waking hour as it was. Every other Sunday she returned to Chicago with no explanation other than that she wanted to be with "family."

By contrast, Gypsy spent a great deal of time feeling hot and sweaty and overworked. Yet she might have got through that dreadful Sunday in mid-July without an explosion if it hadn't been for the washing machine. That was the straw that broke the camel's back.

The day started off badly. Gypsy had begun the summer rising every morning at least a half hour before the others so she could plug in the thirty cup percolator and then have fifteen minutes or so of private meditations. Within days she'd found her personal time nibbled into by tasks that were just so much easier to do before the others got up and in her way. Before long she was making no pretense of using the time for prayer. It was simply a half-hour's jump on the day, and she planned her schedule accordingly. That she was avoiding God, she refused to admit.

On this particular morning, her alarm failed to go off. She wakened at nine-thirty and stared at her clock wild-eyed. She could hear the others up and about and when she groped out into the kitchen a few minutes later she grumbled to Theresa, "Why didn't someone wake me up? You know I have to be in church by ten. Where's Jody?"

"Oh, he went to Peoria with Dayt and Ila. Didn't you know? Ila is going to sing at First Presbyterian this morning. Jode wanted to hear her."

"No! I didn't know!" Gypsy jerked her cup from under the coffee spigot too soon and spilled coffee all down the front of the cabinet. Who did Jody think he was, just running off like that without even asking her permission? Dayt and Ila, Dayt and Ila, her mind sneered. I'm *sick* of hearing their names linked!

Thrown together, she got to church just in time for the collection, opened her purse, and found her billfold empty. Rats! She'd forgotten to get some cash yesterday. During the sermon her mind kept wandering off the minister's words and onto the fact that she'd had to turn down a chance to play for summer services because of her tight schedule. The present organist was adequate. Well, really insipid, Gypsy decided as the congregation droned through the closing hymn at a funeral pace. *I could put some life into that song,* she told herself grouchily. *It's tiresome to just sit here listening to the same ideas I've been hearing all my life. I'd rather be thinking about what I'm going to play next.*

After church, Gypsy hurried home and began work on the brunch she'd planned. While she was grating cheese for quiche, Sandy accosted her.

"Gyps, I don't know what's the matter with the washing machine. Last night I put in a batch of towels and forgot about them; when I checked them just now, the water hadn't drained. The tub's not off-balance; I checked that the first thing."

"Oh, for goodness. . . . Find Mark; he's an electrician; maybe he'll know how to fix it."

Fifteen minutes later, Mark informed her, "Sorry, Gypsy, but I think it's the pump. You'll have to call a repair man for that. Is it still in warranty?"

" 'Still in warranty'?" Gypsy rasped. "Good night, can't you tell by looking at it it's at least fifteen years old? Probably the whole thing's shot!"

"Well, don't take my head off, Gyps. I didn't do it," Mark protested and left.

Dayt dropped off Ila and Jody just as the others were finishing brunch. With the coming of hot weather, Gypsy had put three borrowed picnic tables on the front porch for cooler dining. She gestured impatiently for Jody to come take his place, but he said, "We've had lunch, Gyps. Dayt says we should all get over to his pool, 'cause it's gonna be a scorcher today. Last one into his swimsuit is a rotten egg!"

Shawn, Dan, and Sparky lunged off their benches in playful acceptance of Jody's challenge, and Mark, Sandy, and Theresa, the clean-up squad for the day, began a hurried clearing of the tables.

"Hey! Careful! That's my grandmother's good china you're slapping around there!" Gypsy yelled as Mark piled a treacherously teetering load onto a tray. Next Sunday they'd get cheese sandwiches on paper plates, she silently vowed. No more trying to add a graceful note to the week's end with a special meal and beautiful place settings. Pearls before swine . . .

"Gyps, get your suit on. Aren't you coming?" It was Jody by her side, towel draped around his bare shoulders and champing at the bit to be off for the pool.

Gypsy tried not to sound cross as she replied. "Not right now, Jody. Maybe later. By the way," she said, turning stern eyes on him, "what's the idea of sneaking off to Peoria this morning without even asking me if you could go?"

Jody, sensitive as any early teenager about his child-man status, pulled into himself defensively. "Ila invited me to go. I didn't know I had to take orders from you even on Sunday."

The words were a whip. So that was what she meant to this boy for whom she was changing her life? A dictator?

Her answer was calm but cold. "You are my responsibility, Jody. As long as that's so, I expect you to keep me informed as to your whereabouts."

"It was my fault, Gypsy."

Gypsy spun around. There stood Ila clad in a sea-green maillot and beach robe, her brilliant emerald eyes scornful of Gypsy's anger.

"I asked Jody to come along because he was up and dressed and you were still sleeping. Neither of us had any intention of upsetting you with our simple little excursion to Peoria."

Gypsy didn't trust herself to speak. Jody stood between the two women, a pawn in their subtle contest of wills.

"Go on, go swimming." Gypsy followed her abrupt dismissal of Jody by retreating to the room she shared with Theresa, her cheeks fiery with checked anger. She yanked off her church-going clothes and stepped into her oldest swimsuit, a dilapidated two-piecer she'd formerly worn for sunbathing purposes when no one else was around. She lay down on her bed in front of the window fan, waiting till she was sure everyone had cleared out before she emerged from the hot room. What she needed, she decided, far more than a swimming party at Dayt's, was a few hours of peace and quiet all to herself. I must be getting old, she thought. I used to love the haphazard life of working nights, sitting around with a gang after hours for snacks and coffee, doing my personal chores any time of the day or night I felt like it. Now odd hours, irregular schedules, are driving me crazy!

Theresa came in and changed quickly into her swimsuit, saying nothing more than a swift, "Bye, now," to the disgruntled Gypsy sprawled before the fan.

Gypsy waited until she was sure everyone else had departed, then dragged herself off the bed and out into the living room. It was a mess as usual.

"Yuck! Sunday or no, I can't *stand* to look at this hodge-podge," she griped and passed to the kitchen closet to get the vacuum sweeper. At the kitchen door, she blinked unbelievingly. Not a dish had been washed! The sink counter was covered with stacks of dirty tableware. A note taped to the faucet read, "Gyps: we'll get these when we come back for supper. Too hot for dishwashing right now! Theresa."

Gypsy choked back the naughty words that sprang to her lips. "Too hot? Not too hot to eat all that lovely meal I fixed for you, was it?" she screeched to the invisible offenders. "Not too hot for *me* to try to prepare supper around this jumble!"

Now, wait a minute, she counseled herself, it's just dishes; no harm will come from their sitting around dirty a few hours—except the sterling will tarnish, of course. I guess I probably left dishes in the sink a few times when I wanted to do something else. I'll clear one spot and make the chef's salad for tonight's supper, then go cool off on the porch.

She opened the refrigerator to get out her salad supplies—there were none. Whose duty was it to tend the garden yesterday?

She checked the list. Sparky's. That bubble-head! She was the very one who'd requested chef's salad for tonight!

Gypsy sighed and got out the produce basket. She trudged out to the garden, which she hadn't seen for a week or more, thanks to her overloaded schedule. Weeds had conquered the kingdom! The rain on Monday coupled with warm nights and hot days since had fed the monsters to prodigious strength. Gypsy began to sort through the rank invaders for the vegetables she had so lovingly planted, slapping at the hordes of insects disturbed when she rustled through their weedy homes. Sweat poured down her face, her back, between her breasts, enticing even more biters. She yanked ruthlessly at lettuce, peppers, tomatoes, onions, growing steamier with every pull. In her mind's eye, she could see the company over at Dayt's, frolicking in the cool heaven of his pool, or lolling in skimpy-suited ease at one of the green-and-white umbrella tables. Ila would look sensational in a maillot; her long legs and golden-tanned skin were made for showing off. And Dayt—well, she remembered the taut-bodied splendor of his rugged physique encumbered only with swim trunks. That summer she'd spent at his pool she'd marveled every time he'd risen out of the water, a Greek god to her infatuated eyes.

She straightened, brushed a straggle of damp hair out of her eyes, and readjusted the irritatingly saggy bra straps that kept falling down to bind her upper arms. Might as well wash these vegetables off in the aged basement sink where threshermen used to clean up in the old days. It would be cooler there. Besides, the kitchen sink was full of dishes.

Once in the basement, some devil prompted her to check the washing machine after she'd dumped the vegetables into the sink. Gypsy lifted the washer lid and let out a barnyard epithet she kept in reserve for only the pitiest of pits. Sandy hadn't wrung out the load by hand and dried it like any responsible person would! A tub full of towels from Gypsy's none-too-generous supply sat in cold, soap-scummy water, pathetically unready for the wet bodies they'd be expected to dry tonight.

That did it! Gypsy literally saw red as she rammed up the stairs two at a time and tore into her room to find a work shirt of Gramps's to cover her ratty swimsuit.

Gypsy flinched from the hot plastic upholstery of her old Maverick, but it didn't stop her from grinding into gear and boiling off for Dayt's like a mad hornet.

The temper she thought she'd subdued into moderation blazed out like a cannon at the injustice of her situation. Here she was, working herself half to death for a bunch of ungrateful, selfish leeches who saw nothing beyond their own needs. And what did she get for it? Ila's cool-eyed superiority, Jody's designation as tyrant, and Dayt's flagrant encouragement to all the rebels. Well, this was the day of reckoning! No more Miss Nice Gal!

She gunned up the lane to O'Rourke Farms and screeched to a rock-splattering halt behind the New Earth van. As she jumped out of her car, her shirttail caught on the door handle, ripping out the entire back shoulder seam, but she didn't pause to note it. She strode around the house to the wooden-fenced pool enclosure from whence came carefree shouts and splashings that further incensed her fury. She grabbed the gate handle and burst into the pool area like an avenging angel.

A hot game of water volleyball was in progress and nobody noticed her except Dayt and Ila, who, as she might have expected, were lounging at an umbrella table some distance from the pool's edge, iced-tea glasses in hand.

Dayt half rose from his chair, "Gypsy? What's the—"

"Jody!" Gypsy screamed, "get out of that pool and come home with me right now!"

Jody, right in the thick of the game, turned startled eyes on her. The wrath in her voice was unmistakable.

"What's wrong, Gyps?" he asked, puzzled.

The others turned to look at her now, wiping pool water out of their eyes and staring at her disheveled appearance.

"What's wrong," she ground out in nearly breathless anger, "is that I'm surrounded by irresponsible ingrates! While you're all over here having fun, I've been home trying to pick up the pieces left by a pack of hoity-toity 'artists' who are too good to do grubby old menial labor! So you'll have to come home and help me, Jody, if there's to be any supper tonight, dishes to eat off, or towels to dry with. Not to mention a garden that'll have to be weeded before we have to start eating burdock and Creeping Charlie! Unless, of course, *Mr.* O'Rourke and *Dr.* Danova have been sitting over there figuring out some way to get all these things done by magic!"

"Now, see here, Gypsy! You've got no call to come over here and talk like that!" Dayt was at her side, anger spilling out of his ocean-stormy eyes. "Just because you're in a snit over something—"

"'Something'? You call the mess I just left behind a mere 'something'? Reva was right; she said she'd be nuts to take on the care and feeding of a bunch of actors!"

"Gypsy!" Dayt grabbed her shoulders with hurting forcefulness. "You calm down right now! You insisted on taking on this job, and you're not going to pull your spoiled brat act on my guests. You don't seem to remember all the times your grandmother did your chores while you were having fun at the piano, do you?"

Oh, that was low! To call her a spoiled brat in front of all

126

these people, especially Jody. And Ila. The steam nearly shot out of her head, and the impulse to shove him into the pool was well-nigh irresistible.

"Don't you try it, you little fury, or you'll wish you hadn't!" Dayt could see her intentions.

Gypsy stepped back, as if relenting, and he relaxed his grip on her shoulders.

Ila rose from her chair. "Why didn't you tell us how all this was building up, Gypsy, instead of storing it to ruin our afternoon off? Come, Jody, all of you, we'll go see to these matters immediately."

"No, Ila, I want you to stay, all of you—" Dayt began, but Ila, queenlike, put her arm around Jody's shoulders and started for the gate.

"Thank you, Dayton. Another time. I'll wait for you in the van," she called to the bewildered swimmers straggling out of the pool and finding their towels. "The house will be perfect when you get back, Gypsy," she intoned coolly.

"Good. You'll find your supper in the basement sink," Gypsy snapped, unrepentant to the core. She and Dayt stood glaring at each other as the guests filed out, and the van rolled away. Then Dayt took a step toward her, jaw jutting belligerently. With one quick thrust, Gypsy darted into him, shoving him back and over the brink of the pool. His roar mingled with a huge splash as he hit the water. Gypsy wheeled to run for the gate. She couldn't believe how fast he came charging out of the water as she fumbled, scared, at the gate handle. Just as his wet hand grabbed her shoulder, she let out a piercing shriek. Stilettolike pain was stabbing just under her left shoulder blade.

"Ahh! Ahh!" she screamed, dancing in agony and

clawing at her back, trying to reach the red hot needle boring again and again into her flesh. "My back! Something's on my back!"

"It's a wasp!" One of Dayt's steely arms caught her around the waist to hold her still while his hand ripped the back out of the shirt and grasped the wasp that was injecting its venom into her in a sickening parody of her own recent outburst. She heard the crunch of the wasp's body under Dayt's bare heel. A wave of nausea swept her; she was so hot, so upset, and now pain throbbed demonlike all the way up to her neck.

"Gypsy! Are you allergic to stings?" Dayt demanded, shaking his thick wet mop of blond hair to clear his eyes.

"No, I don't think so," Gypsy moaned, fighting to hold back the vomit rising in her throat. "But, oh . . . it hurts!"

He swept her up into his arms. "I've got to put something on those stings! Don't struggle, Gypsy, just let me get you into the house!" He barged out through the gate and rushed up the stone walk to the house.

"Down . . . put me down . . . just a minute," she choked out.

Dayt set her down and she staggered off a few feet before her stomach forcibly relieved itself. She wiped off her mouth with the tail of her shirt and turned to find Dayt right there to half walk, half carry her into the house.

"I'm sorry—such a mess—" she apologized, stumbling against him. "Ugh!"

He opened the door and they stepped into the mercy of air conditioning. "I've seen lots worse things than that, honey. All I'm worried about is a possible reaction to the venom; that's serious business, you know." He led her through his bedroom to his bath, where he opened the medicine chest. "I've got some antisting stuff that ought to help a little. Turn around, Gypsy. Take off your shirt or what's left of it!"

He spread the soothing ointment over the aching nodules on her back, then led her out to his bed. "Just sit here, baby, and let the salve take effect. I'm going to get out of this wet suit, and then I'll be back to take care of you." He patted her arm and stepped into his bathroom.

Gypsy sat with eyes closed and felt the tears backing up behind the lids. What a witch she had been! She began to cry, weak from wrath, pain, and regret. And Dayt's kindness—somehow it hurt worse than if he'd told her off, told her she'd got just what she deserved, tearing into his party and breaking it up with a tantrum.

Dayt came out of the bathroom, dried off and in jeans and an unbuttoned cotton shirt. "Gyps! What's the matter? Are you still sick?" His concern hurried him to the bed.

She shook her head morosely, lips bound together to stop her sniveling. "I'm just . . . tired. And ashamed. Dayt . . ." She turned her eyes, violet pools of pain, up to his. "Please don't hate me. I'm *so* ashamed."

A warmth, a return of the friendliness she so treasured, smoothed his brows. He chuffed a light breath of surrendered anger. "Oh, hey . . . how could I hate you? Get mad at you? Yeah, that's easy. But hate?"

Somewhat shakily, she started to rise; he pulled her up gently to stand in the circle of his arms, tucked under his chin and into the broad, tawny-haired chest rising and falling in calm strength.

"Poor little Gypsy-girl," he muttered into the dark mass

of her hair. "It's just one crisis after another, isn't it?" His cheek massaged her throbbing forehead while her tears spurted anew. "I hate to say, 'I told you so,' but—"

"I know," she gulped, pulling back to wipe at her eyes, "but . . . you told me so!" Without thinking she reached up to brush the moisture glistening the skin where her face had lain, but her hand snatched back before she made contact. His brow twitched; a small grin followed her exclamation, "Oh, dear . . . this is the *second* time I've blubbered all over you!"

"Who's complaining? This is a lot more pleasant than being on the receiving end of one of your tirades. But we'll get to that later. Right now I want you to take a nice, cool shower, after which I'll reapply the ointment and then you can lie down in my bed for a long nap."

"Oh, no, Dayt, I can't do that! I've got to get home and—"

He stopped her, saying decisively, "You'll do as I say, Mary Catherine. You're exhausted; your eyes look like two black holes of Calcutta and your body . . . " one hand rippled down her rib cage, "feels like you haven't had a full meal in weeks. So hustle on into the shower before I throw you in myself. I *owe* you one, you know!" he shot back good-naturedly.

Gypsy managed to laugh, remembering the outraged bull who'd come roaring out of the pool. "Well, if you insist," she acquiesced, trying to step back out of range of a physical attraction so powerful it drew her like a lodestone. "But I'll spare you the sight of my skinny body and take my own shower, thank you."

A derisive snort and a playful pat on her backside

accompanied his comment, "There's nothing wrong with your body a few good meals . . . and maybe a few good babies . . ." he stuck in as an afterthought, "wouldn't cure." He laughed again at her quick headsnap on the "babies" suggestion and sauntered over to a dresser. "Here, Punkin," he quipped, opening a drawer, "I suppose you're the type to go formal." He threw her the obviously never-worn top to some pajamas and grinned at her awkward clutch at them.

She tried to think of some witty retort, but her tongue seemed all a-wobble. She ducked her head and fled to the bathroom.

While lukewarm water coursed over her, relaxing all her body except the hard knots where the wasp had done its foul work, she willed herself to see Dayt's actions and remarks for just what they were—kindnesses meant to lighten her mood and pull the sting of jealous poison that had turned her into a harridan. But when he touched her—She toweled off, forcing her mind away from the shimmery threads of awareness that sang every time she came near Dayt.

She buttoned herself into the pajama top that reached nearly to her knees. Then she stood regarding her modestly covered figure in the mirror running the length of the lavoratory counter. Now she had to go out and pretend that climbing into his bed, albeit alone, meant nothing more to her than a chance to catch up on her sleep. I can't do it! she fretted.

"Gyps? You all right?" Dayt's voice from the other side of the door reminded her that she'd been in the bath a rather long time for a simple shower.

"Yes! Coming!" she called back and snatched up a comb to run through her soaked hair. She wrapped another towel around her head to protect the pillow, took a deep breath, and emerged into the bedroom. Her eyes slid immediately to the king-sized bed where Dayt had turned back the covers. He waited beside it, ointment in hand.

"Come on, Punkin, let Daddy fix your 'owie,'" he joked and sat on the edge of the massive bed.

Gypsy resisted an urge to wet her dry lips; she walked slowly to sit beside him, turned, and waited for his ministrations. He pulled her pajama collar away from her neck so that his tough, tender fingers could reach in and gently smooth a coat of salve over the still-painful stings. Under the folds of her generous nightshirt she clenched her hands into fists to stop the tremble that would have given away her shuddery delight in his soft stroking.

"There you go," he said, pulling her collar back into place. "Now, down under the covers for a good rest, Gyps. Oh, by the way, I called over to your place to tell them what happened, just in case they thought we murdered each other or something."

"Oh . . . thanks," she murmured. She hesitated a fraction of a second, her eyes fluttering away from his, then scooted back and slipped under the fine percale sheets to settle on the down pillow. The faintest trace of his after shave clung there. "Dayt . . ." she offered tentatively, "I . . . I truly am sorry for the way I acted. I—" She couldn't finish.

His aspect turned solemn. "You should be," he agreed reflectively. "I'm telling you, Gyps: if you don't get that rash temperament under control, you're going to make yourself a hell on earth." He paused, as if pondering

132

whether to say what came next. "Gypsy." He took her hand in his. "Have you ever considered asking the Lord to help you with this? He could, you know."

Gypsy stirred, uneasy. When had Dayt taken to promoting the Lord? He hadn't been trammeled by any overabundance of sanctity a few years ago, to that she could attest. "I . . . suppose so." She looked up at him, hopeful. "I know *you* could help me, Dayt. You always do, when I slow down and let you."

His response wasn't what she'd expected. His jaw pulled awry in disturbed hesitancy before he said, "Gypsy, I'm not God." The ponderousness of his declaration apparently struck him a bit humorously, because he laughed and modified his stance with, "I'm pretty wonderful, I know, but . . . but don't get a bumbling, egocentric human being confused with God."

She didn't know what to reply; she lay, slightly flushed, looking up into his serious gaze with puzzled eyes.

"Hey—we'll talk about this heavy stuff after you've had a good sleep," he veered off suddenly. He unwrapped the towel from her hair. "You can't rest with that wad on your noggin," he pronounced, throwing the damp cloth over a chair.

"But I'll get your pillow all wet!" she protested, glad for a break in a conversation that was disturbing her.

"So what? I'll throw it into the dryer. Sleep tight, Toots." For just a second she thought he was going to kiss her, but instead he left abruptly, closing the solid oak door to protect her privacy.

Little by little Gypsy let her tight-coiled muscles unwind against the silky-cool sheets. She didn't understand Dayt's worrying that she might mistake him for God; what did he mean by that? What she did know was that the bed and the room were heavenly cool, the pillow soft to her achy head. She was safe—that was it—safe, protected from every-thing, even her blast furnace temper, because Dayt was on the other side of that door. What did she need of anyone else if she had him? She turned her face into the downy pillow and let herself wash away in deep, dreamless sleep.

chapter

7

"GYPSY? HONEY?" A voice, soft but masculine, was calling from a long distance. Gypsy stirred, hugging the extra pillow she'd somehow got into her arms, and was aware of a body next to hers. But where was she?

"Gypsy? Can you wake up?"

It was Dayt's voice. Her eyes opened slowly to a darkened room; she felt a man's hand caress her cheek and she turned over, blinking at the faint glow of light from the hallway.

"Oh, Dayt! Oh, my goodness; how long have I slept?"

Dayt was stretched out on top of the covers, shoulders propped against the headboard. He smiled down at her and brushed her hair back from her face. "About seven hours. It's ten-thirty."

"Ten-*thirty*?" Gypsy bounded up in bed. "It *can't* be!"

"Well, it is, Punkin, and you must have needed that sleep desperately. I hated to wake you, but it's time for your feeding."

"My 'feeding'? Now, Dayt, you make me feel like a baby! How—long have you been sitting—uh—lying there?"

"Long enough to decide you looked like a sweet little

kitten, all curled up here sleeping like there's no tomorrow." His voice hoarsened with tender teasing. "Looks sure can be deceiving, can't they?" he taunted and tweaked a sprig of her tousled locks.

"Mmf!" she grinned shyly and squirmed, self-conscious.

"Turn over and let me give you one more dab of salve, then I'll find you some suitable dinner clothes."

She turned slowly, as he requested, hitching the shirt back from her shoulders to allow the careful pressure of his fingers on her soft skin.

"I threw your swimsuit into the washer while you were sleeping, and it just sort of . . . disintegrated. I hope it wasn't something you hated to throw away?"

"Hardly," she laughed. "I guess I kept it out of habit. I have others."

"Good. I don't want to hear you're running around skinny dipping, at least not unless it's with me!"

She giggled outright at his kidding. "Fat chance! What have you got for me to wear?"

He got off the bed and rummaged in his dresser. "Here, Modesty. They'll be too big, but it's the best I can do." He tossed her a pair of white running shorts, then got a blue cotton shirt from his closet. "There are safety pins in the top dresser drawer if you need 'em. See you on the patio in five minutes for steaks and salad. Don't be late."

He ambled out of the room, leaving Gypsy to arrange herself in his attire. She tied the monstrously large shirt into a tummy knot and rolled the sleeves to mid-arm.

At the patio door she paused, brought up short by an entrancing scene. Full moonlight filtered down through an opening in the giant oaks to burnish Dayt's lustrous hair and lean figure. He was standing at the gas grill, busied with the final moments of steak tending. To his right an old-fashioned barn lantern hung on a pole, softly illuminating a white wrought iron table set with red stoneware and Waterford crystal. A magnificent white gladiola floated in a clear crystal bowl in the center of the red and white linened table.

Pleasure swept Gypsy. This was beautiful, and it was for *her*! Dayt had replaced her drudging, sweat-mopped existence with cool, clean, delicious pampering that made her feel womanly, even in his clothes. He gave a steak one last flip and the brown, savory aroma awakened hunger that seemed to reach her very toes.

"Dayt, this is terrific! I'm starved!" she exclaimed, coming quickly to stand by him and cast hankering glances at the steaks sizzling sassily in their rich juices. "I didn't know you were a chef," she bantered.

He gave her a comrade's grin, but his swift, approving survey of her slender figure in his personal attire jolted her vulnerable self-containment.

"A somewhat limited chef, Gypsy. This is pretty much my stock-in-trade entertainment menu. Stay one more night and you either eat the same thing, or we go out for dinner!" He used tongs to lift two foil-wrapped potatoes to the waiting red plates.

"Oh." Gypsy swerved away, reminded in a flash of all the women besides herself he must have "entertained" just as gallantly—all the ones who'd probably stayed far longer than one night. Including . . . Ila?

She stepped to the dinner table, hiding her temporary letdown by opening the potatoes and topping them with butter.

"Well, I've become the undisputed mistress of hamburger improvisation," she quipped with forced lightness. "'A thousand and one ways to disguise hamburger in a main dish,' that's *my* specialty."

"I know." He picked up a crystal pitcher to pour two glasses of lemonade. "That's something we have to discuss," he said, handing her a sparkling goblet, "but not before we cut into these steaks—"

"Why? Has someone—Ila?—been complaining about my cooking?" she shot out, immediately on guard.

He stopped the hoisting of his own glass midway. "No." His eyes raked the semidarkness, searching for hers. "Gypsy, what's this big chip you've got on your shoulder concerning Ila? Why are you so antagonistic toward her?" There was accusation in the question.

Her head tossed away from his inquisition. How could she tell him the truth, that it made her sick to share his attentions with the auburn-haired director, that her thoughts sometimes conjured images of an intimacy between him and Ila unbearable to her quickened heart?

"It's . . . nothing," she fibbed, eyes averted. "I just get a little tired of her . . . aloofness—I don't know—her air of . . . superiority?" she stumbled, trying to find a description of Ila's offenses that wouldn't incriminate herself.

"That's how you see her?" he probed slowly, a troubled note darkening his tone. "Gypsy, Ila is a woman of faith. What you call 'aloofness' or 'superiority'—she's anchored in Christ; it makes her the most self-disciplined woman I've ever known."

"And I'm the least?" Gypsy couldn't stop the question even though she knew the answer would hurt. How blind he was! Ila could afford to be self-controlled; she seemed to have no one in the world to worry about except herself, and she had Dayt to do most of that for her! "I'm some kind of infidel?" Gypsy persisted.

He didn't immediately reply; she could see disappointment cloud his expression. He sipped his lemonade, considering. "I don't know for sure all that you are." He sipped again, never taking his eyes from hers. Then a conciliatory smile caught up a corner of his mouth. "But the steaks are burning while we stand here dabbling in character analysis." Part of his old-time roguery returned to imp his widening grin. "Let's just say you're the cutest little kitten ever to snuggle down in my bed."

Heat flooded her face. Ila was a saint, but she was a—a plaything? "I don't intend to enter *that* competition!" she snapped. Her glass clattered, untasted, onto a nearby wrought iron end table, and she turned in abrupt irritation to leave.

"Hold on, Spitfire!" Dayt's commanding grip captured her shoulders and prevented her escape; amusement vied with anger in his manner. "Would you be happier if I failed to appreciate what I *do* know of your character, the passionate side? I'm no fool, Gypsy."

Anger, hurt, confusion rushed in on her, rocketing her temper into high gear. "You've had plenty of experience, so I'm sure you know the signs!"

He opened his mouth, closed it quickly, took a deep breath. "There's such a thing as instinct, you know. I don't sleep around; never have."

"Oh, yeah. Right. And all those girls who used to come down here from Chicago—Girl Scouts, every one of them, I'll bet!"

"Gypsy, stop and think: I've never yet opened my door to a guest that Reva wasn't over here like a shot. Have you ever heard *her* say anything about my messing around?"

"Well . . . no, but—"

He watched with a wry half-smile while she wrestled with that one. There was no need to say that what Reva knew everybody in Sauk Valley soon heard.

"You spend most of your time in Chicago. Are you going to say there's never been anyone there?"

He looked away; it was a second before he replied. "You already know the answer to that. I told you that day in the barn: I had a long, serious relationship with a woman. One of those 'Let's-not-get-married-and-spoil-it' things." He seemed to be far away for a moment. "If you want some advice from an old man, Gyps, listen up. The day you decide to go in for one of those farces, just find yourself a big buzz-saw, throw yourself onto it, and get yourself all cut up fast! Don't prolong the misery!"

A strange, sickish turmoil surged in Gypsy. She wanted desperately to ask more about this liaison; specifically, had it been with Ila? Oh, yes, Ila professed to be a Christian, but maybe she hadn't been one long. Before that—

"Gypsy?"

She looked up into Dayt's inquiring eyes.

"Does that bother you . . . a lot? I mean . . . that I took a long, deliberate fall from grace?"

It was so hard to answer. So hard to realize that whatever had passed between him and Ila in other years, he still found so much in her, so little in Gypsy. Had Ila ever been poor? Ever disrupted her whole life to take in an orphan? Ever toiled away at hard, unglamorous work when she could have been prettily dressed, making music, garnering compliments right and left from pleased listeners? It wasn't fair!

"Yes," she said at last. "It bothers me. A lot." She steadied herself. "But if you now see it as a wrong move, who am I to judge?"

"Gypsy . . ." Dayt leaned down to her, his brows knit in concern. "Don't be upset. Everybody has to learn about at least one of the commandments the hard way—which doesn't excuse me, I know. But I have learned." He led her gently towards a chair. "Now let's have a nice dinner and be friends. There's no one in the world I'd rather see smile than you. Friends?"

His pleading and his gentle fingertip brushing the downturn of her mouth partially stilled her agitation. He *was* trying to give her a pleasurable evening. Her lips relented and followed his lead into a wavery smile. "Sure. Friends."

The hard knot of apprehension gradually dissolved from Gypsy's middle as she toyed with salad dressing and condiments. By the time she lifted the first bite of O'Rourke Farms ribeye to her mouth, she felt able to do justice to the simple, delicious meal Dayt had prepared for her.

"You cook a very fine steak, Ollie," she joked in a laconic Laurel voice to her host, whose eyes, smiling and affectionate—was that the feeling?—seemed to be on her every time she looked toward him.

"Thanks awfully, Stan," he kidded in true Hardy fashion. "May I interest you in a bit more nectar?" With the exaggerated elegance of the master comic, he replenished her glass, sending her into laughter that refreshed like rain. The dining proceeded leisurely with Dayt attentive to her every need.

A breeze, soft and balmy, drifted across the moonlit patio, a tantalizing satin kiss after the simmering day. The tang of Illinois farmland offering up its soul in bumper crops of corn, oats, beans, and hay accented a backdrop of velvety sky, brilliant stars. Far off, cattle lowed, a mournful reproach to some disturbance of their midsummer night's peace.

Gypsy's fork sank to her plate. "This life is beautiful, isn't it?" she murmured, her always-sensitive heart swelling with the charm of these precious moments. "This farm life, I mean."

"Yes." Dayt, too, put aside the last of his meal. After a moment's silence, he slid back his chair and proposed, "Would you like an after-dinner stroll around the premises, Gyps? I can't offer any dessert, just coffee."

"Oh, yes, I'd love to walk, Dayt," she answered honestly. "Your grounds are so handsome."

"Thanks to Reva. She's my landscape artist," Dayt laughed. "And, of course, Jody gets a lot of credit too." He helped her out of her seat, and it seemed perfectly natural for his arm to rest lightly along her shoulders as they began a slow ramble through the oak-filled patio yard, around to the pool side of the house where open space provided plenty of sun for Reva's garden. "I didn't know whether you felt the same way about Sauk Valley life as I do, Gypsy. I mean, you left to wander," Dayt continued as they sauntered along the perimeters of the moon-drenched flower beds.

"I left, but not because I didn't love it here. It's just that Matt Morris came along and offered me a chance to live up to my nickname."

"Ah, yes, the great entrepreneur, Matt Morris." An edginess ringed his remark and he stopped, turning to face her. "That's one of the things I need to talk to you about, Gyps. I ran into him the other day in Chicago. He wants to get in touch with you."

"Yes? You sound like you don't approve of that." Gypsy's curiosity was aroused. She'd always found the thirtyish Matt to be a fair, not to mention attractive, employer.

Dayt examined a rosebush in the bed bordering the pool fence. "Matt's okay. Maybe a shade more interested in his female employees than he ought to be—" He snapped a red blossom from the bush.

"Really? He's certainly never stepped out of line with me," Gypsy defended.

"That's good. Anyway, he says he's got an idea he wants you to hear; probably wants you to go back on the circuit. He said . . . uh . . . you're the most popular entertainer with both customers and management he's ever sent out." The rose twirled between his thumb and forefinger. "To tell the truth, I think he's got a case on you, Gypsy." The last words were only half teasing.

"Umm?" Gypsy leaned to sniff at a blossom. "That's interesting. I don't have that many handsome, intelligent, successful men throwing themselves at my feet," she taunted, hoping to strike just a little spark of jealousy in Dayt, a taste of what she felt every time he praised Ila.

"Yeah?" The displeased monosyllable fulfilled her wish.

143

She pressed her advantage. "And, of course, Matt's always understood—and appreciated—my music for what it is, pure entertainment. He doesn't see that as an unworthy accomplishment."

"Hurray for Matt!"

Dayt's rough annoyance was just what she wanted to hear; she willingly eased off. "But I don't see much point in getting in touch with him. I mean, with Jody, and the farm, and all—"

"Well, I'm just passing on his message. I . . . uh . . . thought after today, his offer might sound pretty good to you. It's obvious you can't go on with the load you've been carrying."

"I'd have to think about it, a long time. The gypsy life—you can grow out of that, you know."

"Can you?"

They stood silently, regarding each other through assessing eyes. Then Gypsy broke the impasse with coaxing. "Come on, Dayt, let's finish our walk." Her hand moved tentatively toward him; he caught it and drew it around his waist.

"Sure, Gyps." Slowly, he pulled her tight to his side, then they resumed their stroll. His arm around her back was tighter, more possessive than it had been earlier. Something new, a growing sensual tension, an expectancy, was filtering, seductive as the moonlight, into their late-night mood, and it thrilled along Gypsy's nerves like a miniature chorus. They drifted back toward the patio.

"Gypsy, if you *could* have just the life you wanted, what would it be?"

The question took her by surprise. The life she wanted?

144

The image of what she longed for—*had* longed for for years—sprang crystal clear to her mind's eye. Five years flipped away as if they'd never occurred and she knew: it had never been infatuation, a silly crush she'd had on him. She'd loved him. To be his wife, to bear his children, to share everything, good or bad, in his life—that's what she wanted.

The realization of her heart's choice made it begin a slow, heavy thudding that sent waves of doubting tenderness undulating through her. "That's a . . . difficult thing to say," she hedged, hard-pressed to get words past the relentless beating in her throat. "What kind of life would *you* have?" she countered.

They were back at the patio; he turned to face her, watching her response to his words. "I'd have a law practice in Peoria so I could live here at O'Rourke Farms full-time. I'd have a wife that I loved as the better half of myself. I'd have children."

She stood stunned, tingling with the frankness of his answer, with the way it meshed with *her* secret dream. "And what . . . are you doing about it?" she dared ask. That Dayton O'Rourke would ever want anything—or anybody—and not go after it was impossible for her to imagine.

"I've already taken action toward part of my goal, Gypsy. I'm closing my Chicago office and moving it to Peoria. By late fall, I'll be a full-time resident at O'Rourke Farms."

"That's . . . that's wonderful, Dayt!" she managed to gasp. "And the rest—?"

"The rest is proving . . . a lot more complicated. But not impossible."

She waited expectantly for him to go on; when he didn't she shifted, disquieted by the tiny threads of attraction that seemed to be pulling her right into his arms. "It . . . uh . . . must be getting awfully late," she finally ventured. "Time for me to go home." She tried to slip around him.

One agile movement, and he'd blocked her path.

"Oh!" She walked right into him. The warmth, the strength of his stalwart presence prickled like an electric shock.

His chuckle was husky, desirous. "First, let me give you something." Light but knowing hands tucked the red rose into her hair above her ear, then coaxed her startled face to turn up to his. "Perfect," he murmured. "Now you're the perfect embodiment of gypsy allure."

"Dayt, really—" She was flustered, breathless with warring impulses. "I'm just Mary Catherine Connor, the underweight boardinghouse keeper from down the road!" She flung the words in a desperate attempt to clear her own senses.

"No. Oh, no," he contradicted, tenderly domineering. His toughened palms slid up her forearms and under the widecuffed shirtsleeves; dexterous fingers began a gentle kneading of her upper arms. "You're far more than that. You're Gypsy, tantalizing, exasperating, follow-your-own-star Gypsy. And—" His eyes darkened to midnight blue; the pulse in his throat sped to visible throbbing. "I . . . don't want you to go just yet."

"I . . . I don't *want* to go," she fumbled, "but—"

"I gave you something—a rose. Now I want a return gift." His lips, perilously close to hers, descended further to brush the soft, rounded warmth of her mouth. "Come into the house long enough to play one song, one Gypsy-melody for me," he entreated, a breath away from her yearning lips.

Danger! The warning slashed across her consciousness, but too much of her wanted to comply, wanted to fall under the hypnotic spell of Dayton O'Rourke's charisma.

"Wh—what should I play?" she whispered above the pounding of her heart.

Soft as down his kisses blessed her temples, then her lowered eyelids.

"Whatever you think the night—and I—deserve." A tremor passed through him, into her arms, straight on to her agitated breast. "Just one song, Gypsy; that's all I ask."

"Yes." The affirmation spoke for itself.

Like two dreamwalkers, arms locked around each other's waists, they entered the house lighted only by the moon-light streaming in through the many generous windows now opened to the fresh night air. Gypsy sank onto the piano bench, and Dayt leaned into the curve of the great instrument. She could feel the force of his longing as surely as if he'd wrapped her in his embrace. The two of us, she marveled, we both want the same things. He wants to love me; I can tell he does.

She sat for a moment waiting for inspiration. Then she knew what to play. "For you, Dayton," she offered, barely above a whisper, "and for the night."

Her left hand began the slow, sonorous opening meas-ures of Beethoven's "Moonlight Sonata," one of the few classical compositions she'd ever taken the trouble to memorize note for note. It flowed from her fingers in a shimmery evocation of love. She played as she had sung at

Gramps's funeral, expressing her love in a richness of nuance that permeated the very air. Only this love was not the kind she'd had for Gramps, that of a daughter. This was the full, needing, desiring love of a woman for a man—*her* man.

As the beautiful rendition moved toward its crescendo, Gypsy's heart cried endlessly, I love him! I love him!

The last note sounded. She sat, unmoving, overwhelmed by the outpouring of her emotions.

Dayt's dark silhouette moved slowly toward her. Gently he pulled her into his arms as he tenderly kissed her throat and then teasingly caressed her neck. Cupping her face in his palm, he brushed her trembling lips with feathery kisses.

"It's not the grief now, is it, Gypsy?" he whispered, heavy-throated with desire.

"No . . ." she sighed. "Oh, no! It's not the grief!" Her arms came up around his neck, and she eagerly pressed her lips against his firm mouth, begging for his kiss.

"Gypsy! Oh, Gypsy!" As his mouth passionately claimed hers, she buried her fingers in the luxuriance of his thick, soft hair, and such an intense desire overwhelmed her that she seemed helpless to push herself away from him.

When his mouth finally released hers, she said breathlessly, "Dayt—please—we mustn't—"

"Don't say anything, Gypsy, let me hold you the way I've wanted to from the day you came home!" Running his fingers through her hair, glorying in its rich softness, he kissed her again and again.

"Please!" She tried to pull away, to think straight. "We have to stop right now!"

"I know . . . " he murmured, "but—"

"Oh, I know! I know! But I . . . *can't* do that—" The words tore themselves out of her.

"I know you can't, sweetheart," he said, gently kissing her hands, "and neither can I. But times like these I almost want to forget everything. These beautiful hands should never do anything but make music. I can't stand it, Gypsy—the thought of you working yourself so hard over at that theater camp. I won't let you go back to that!"

"But Dayt. . . ." She breathed in hurried, half-dazed gasps. "I have to. I made a bargain and I have to live up to it. You said I was lazy, a spoiled brat, but I'm not. What I've wanted, more than anything else, is for you to see that I've changed; I don't look for the easy way out any more."

"Gypsy, honey—" His voice was incredulous. "You mean you've gone through all this torment just to prove something to *me*?"

With a small, quivering voice she answered, hoping for his understanding. "I would do anything, Dayt, to make you look up to me the way you do to Ila."

Trouble spread across his countenance. "Gypsy . . . baby . . . sweetheart . . ." He floundered in frustration. "Don't you see?" he anguished. "Ila doesn't try to please me or any other human, that is, she doesn't try *first* to do that. She tries to please God. And I respect her for that."

"Don't you think *I* try to please God? I follow the Ten Commandments; I go to church. And for you, Dayt," she pleaded, "I'd change my life in any way you thought I should to measure up to your idea of a good Christian—"

"Gypsy!" His voice tensed with conflict. "You're tempting me to something even worse than . . . you're offering me power over your *soul*. That's wrong, honey!" He strode away a few feet, then turned, hand massaging the back of his neck. "I can't carry that burden; no human could."

She sprang to his side, impelled by her love to break through his argument. "I don't understand you, Dayt. One minute you're bossing me around, telling me what I will or will not do; the next you're pushing me away, talking crazy about 'power over my soul' and . . . and I don't know what-all. If you still think the last thing you need is a romantic involvement with me, just come right out and say so."

She anxiously watched Dayt's tortured features as his gentle hands rested on her slender arms.

"Honey, all I'm trying to get you to see is that I'm qualified to make business decisions for you; I'm *not* qualified to manage your soul. You've got to turn that job over to God."

"All right," she promised impetuously, "I'll do that. You'll see; I'll become the most all-out Christian you've ever known!"

He started to say something, then stopped, expelling a baffled charge of breath. "Gyps—Christianity—it's not a club you join; you can't just follow a bunch of rules and then say, 'Look, I'm a great Christian!' There's much more to it—" He broke off. "But this isn't the time or place to discuss it. We've got to get out of here, let our heads clear. I'm going to take you home, *right now*. Someone can come over tomorrow and pick up your car."

They walked out of the living room. As she felt his hand tighten on her arm, they hesitated and turned to each other, then without a word continued to the front door and out to the car.

Once inside her house, Dayt stated firmly that before he left for Chicago later today, he'd have household help on the way to Gypsy. Tenderly he kissed her with an aching desire that was answered in her lips.

"I'll be back Friday night," he promised against her soft cheek, "and we'll go out to dinner, somewhere in Peoria, where we can talk privately and still keep control. Being alone with you sort of fogs up my will power! Friday, at seven?"

"Yes. Oh, yes, Dayt! I'll be ready!" She knew now that he felt more for her than just desire by the tenderness of his eyes, of his hands tracing the contours of her face. He would return her love, she was certain.

chapter
8

"I'M SORRY, DEEPLY SORRY, for the way I behaved yesterday." Gypsy stood before the New Earthers and Jody as they assembled at the lunch tables. "I was judging you for the same kind of thoughtlessness I've exhibited enough times myself; I ask your forgiveness." With the same impulsiveness that made her flare in anger, Gypsy made her generous apology, willing to forget the whole incident in the wonder of her new love.

The diners stirred restlessly and looked at one another, embarrassed by words of contrition from one who'd had a right to tongue-lash them.

Theresa spoke. "What's there to forgive, Gypsy? I can't think of many people who'd be as patient with a pack of 'hoity-toity artists' as you've been."

"That's right, Gypsy," Shawn agreed, and the others, with the exception of Ila, chimed in their appreciation for her helpfulness. Ila had left early that morning in the van, leaving Mark in charge for the day, with no explanation other than to say she'd be home that evening. No one had questioned her; Gypsy noticed that Ila's reserve kept the New Earthers aware that they answered to her, not the other way around. Gypsy had wanted to make a private apology to her, but that would have to wait.

In the meantime, she began, for the first time, to get some real fun out of her theatrical venture. Now that the company was going to be scrupulous in attending to its household duties, now that a new washing machine churned away happily in the basement, and now that Reva Thompson was to come every day to assist Gypsy, she felt free to accept the players' warm invitation to come out to the barn and see what was going on. Gypsy wasn't thrilled about having the sharp-tongued Reva around, but she was still so totally bemused by last night she'd have accepted Dracula's mother, if that was whom Dayt had sent!

"Gypsy, since Ila's not here, would you sit in on the piano today?" Mark requested. "There are two or three chorus numbers we need to hit hard."

"Sure, Mark," Gypsy readily agreed. "Only—if you need a key change, you'll have to show me what note to start on!" she gaily reminded him, far too hopeful of her future to be longer distressed by her lapse in musical education.

"Will do," Mark promised, and handed her the score for the afternoon rehearsal.

For the next few hours Gypsy was immersed in what she liked to do best, making music. The endless repetitions of difficult choral passages or tricky dance steps weren't boring to her; she was fascinated by the gradual metamorphosis of cocooned ideas into colorful butterflies of performance. She hated to tear herself away to prepare supper, and as soon as it was over she went right back to the barn for further rehearsal. Things were moving along in high gear at eight o'clock when she heard a familiar voice at her shoulder.

"You're doing well; thanks for taking over for me."

It was Ila. Gypsy turned around, meaning to explain why she now had a little time to devote to the artistic end of the barn theater, but Ila's face and bearing stopped her. For the first time in their acquaintance, Gypsy saw fatigue—indeed, a kind of sad weariness—drooping Ila's usually vital frame, shadowing her eyes with dark circles.

"Ila, are you all right?" Gypsy asked, alarmed.

"Yes, I just need some—rest," Ila answered slowly. She looked up at the thespians, halted right in the middle of the final number. "Go on; you're doing just fine. I'll see you all in the morning." To Gypsy she said, "I'd appreciate it very much if you'd stand by me at the piano for the last play. I—may have to be gone at unexpected times."

"Well—yes, Ila—" Gypsy stammered. She wanted to apologize for the previous day's behavior and get things between them on a better footing, but Ila's manner suggested that she was distracted by something to the extent she didn't even remember the unfortunate incident at Dayt's pool. Gypsy decided to let the matter drop, at least for the time being.

"There's some sandwiches in the fridge, left from supper, if you're hungry," she offered kindly.

"Thank you. Perhaps I'll have one later. Good night." Ila walked slowly out of the barn.

Mark called out, "Okay, kids, let's give this one more try and then call it quits for the night. Ready? *One* and two and *three* and four and *five*—"

The players swung into the last run-through of their big number.

A strange week it was for Gypsy: speedy, in that every day was packed with work and rehearsal—she had to attend often if she were going to fill in occasionally for Ila—but slow, for the knowledge that five whole days had to pass before she'd see Dayt dragged like an anchor at her consciousness. He called her every night at supper time. She hung on his words, although they were mostly inquiries about what she'd been doing, or information on his own work.

"I'm swamped," he declared on Wednesday night. "I'm still at the office and probably will be till midnight. A lot of loose ends I'm trying to tie up."

"Oh?" She twined a sprig of hair in anxiety. "They won't keep you from coming back Friday, will they?"

"No way, honey!" he promised fervently. "I hope—I *pray*—Gypsy, that you and I can get our relationship on the right track. It means more to me than you can imagine."

Gypsy closed her eyes, breathless with love and expectation. "Oh, I'm changing every hour, Dayt! I haven't blown up once this week; I'm trying, really hard, to treat everyone fairly. I'm in control of myself. You'll see!" she whispered into the phone. Privacy was in short supply with people popping in and out of the kitchen, cleaning up after the meal. *Please, Lord,* she silently prayed, *if you're really a kind God, let him love me!*

"I'm glad to hear that, Gyps." Was that uncertainty in his remark? "We'll talk all about that Friday night. That and other things. Good night, sweetheart. If I were there right now—" He left the thought unspoken.

Gypsy's enthralled imagination saw the two of them

155

together, holding and kissing each other like last Sunday night.

"Good night, Dayt," she breathed. As soon as she could, she went to her room and read, diligently, page after page from her Bible. If she tried hard enough, surely she'd find her way back to faith. Dayt would lead her, in spite of his unfounded qualms about "managing" her soul.

The next day, while Reva, tall, fortyish, and good-looking in a spare sort of way, put the finishing touches to a spic-and-span living room, she informed Gypsy, "I put that sewing machine in the hall closet. If I find it out when I come back tomorrow, there'll be the dickens to pay! There's no sense, girl, in letting those actor-people live like hogs. Just lay down the law; tell them they can either keep things neat or get out! That's what I'd do."

I'm sure of that, Gypsy thought. Reva wasn't a bad person; it was just that she lived to keep everything around her immaculately clean, uncomfortably clean, clean to the point of obsession. I wonder what the Lord thinks about that kind of life dedication? Gypsy mused.

"I'll do my best, Reva, but I understand their devotion to their art. Have you ever seen them perform? They try to carry God's message in everything they do."

"Huh!" That was Reva's considered opinion of any God-messages not delivered from a pulpit. "Well, that does it for today, Gypsy. I'll be back tomorrow to get that garden whipped into shape. You'll not have a thing to can or freeze if you let those 'artists' muddle around in it. Too bad *weeds* aren't edible; that's what you've got a bumper crop of."

"Uh . . . you don't have to come every day, Reva. I'm

sure it must be a hardship to leave your own work—" Gypsy hoped, desperately, that Reva wouldn't be around, griping, *every* day.

"Oh, I can stand it. What's left of the season? Four, five weeks?"

"About six. The last performance will be Labor Day weekend."

"Next summer they'll have the new building up. It'll be a lot easier to take care of these actors in a regular dormitory instead of this old house." Reva was putting away the cleaning equipment, but Gypsy, brought up sharp, came around to face her.

"What new building? What are you talking about?"

"Why . . ." Reva's brows raised slightly. "Don't you know? It's your property . . . or will be by then. You mean Dayt and Miss High-and-Mighty haven't let you in on their plans?" Reva didn't like Ila; she always referred to her by some unflattering title.

Gypsy tried not to show her surprise. "Why, I've been so busy I haven't even thought about next summer," she began, but her mind was strangely unsettled by her neighbor's revelation. Whatever else she was, Reva was no carrier of false tales. "I, uh—where did you hear this?" Gypsy suddenly demanded.

"Sunday, before you came over and busted up the party," Reva answered promptly.

"*You* know about that?" Gypsy's face burned at the remembrance of her "witch act."

"Sure." Reva neatly folded her dust cloths and stashed them in the ever-present laundry basket waiting to be carried to the basement. "I was working in the flower bed right next to Dayt's pool fence," she went on matter-of-factly, "and I could hear him quizzing Miss H. and M. all about how things were going here—"

"And she answered what?" Gypsy wanted to know, angry with herself for listening to Reva's eavesdropped information, but unable to let it go.

"Well." Reva fixed Gypsy with a wry grin. "You've heard the expression 'Damned with faint praise'?"

Gypsy nodded yes.

"I'd say that's what she was up to. According to her, the food is 'adequate,' the accommodations 'reasonably comfortable.' She didn't say the lack of air conditioning was miserable, but she mentioned about three times how good it had felt in his nice cool house at lunch time."

"Oh . . . they ate at his house?" A pang, a twisted sort of pain, jabbed into Gypsy's heart.

"Uum-huh. Dayt had me fix things the day before, salads, baked ham, and so forth. Say, I've got the best new recipe for fresh raspberry cheesecake! It's easy to make and goes a long way—I'll bet your people would love it. And I can give you all the berries you want—"

"That sounds great," Gypsy broke in, not at all interested in fresh raspberry cheesecake. "I'll get a recipe card," she hurried on, and fled to the drawer where she kept such items. "But what about the building you said they were discussing?" She kept her back to Reva, knowing her face must show the sick writhing of her heart.

"Oh . . . well, they were both mighty happy about the good turnouts at Jesse's Barn, and the quality of the apprentices in the program. Let me tell you, Gyps, Ila's got big plans for this thing; expanded season, more students, more permanent company, possibly a dinner theater. And Dayt's just more than encouraging her. He's the one who came up with the idea of a new dormitory-type building to house the actors. They were just getting into that when you came buzzing in."

Gypsy turned around, her face aflame over that incident, and upset over this reminder of Dayt's close relationship with Ila, not to mention his planning a new facility on *her* property without so much as a by-your-leave.

"I acted like a fool that afternoon, Reva. I'd just as soon forget it."

"Fool? Hmf! I never laughed so hard in my life as I did when you set that bunch straight! The only reason I agreed to come help you, Gyps, is that I admired your gumption in telling them off, especially Miss H. and M. Now you just stay tough around here and you'll get them shaped up fast!" On that emphatic exhortation, Reva took the recipe card and pen from Gypsy and dashed off her newest culinary triumph.

I'll get this talked out with Dayt tonight when he calls, Gypsy vowed after Reva's departure. Except what am I going to say? I heard by way of an eavesdropper that you have big plans for *my* property? Or, what rankles just as much, you dared entertain an old friend at lunch, chaperoned by my teenage ward? That really sounds steamy, doesn't it? Come off it, Gypsy, she chided herself, don't approach Dayton O'Rourke with hearsay or jealousy, or you can say good-by to your chances with him. Better turn your energies toward tonight's supper.

Lightning of the theatrical variety struck Jody on this particular day. When Gypsy went out to the barn to get him for table duty, he sauntered over to her to say in as nearly a Dayt-mannish voice as possible, "I won't be able to set the table tonight, Gyps; Ila's going to give me a special coaching session. But I traded with Dan; I'll wash dishes after supper."

"Oh? And, pray tell, why are *you* getting a coaching session?" Gypsy wondered.

"Jimmy Tate, that apprentice from Shawana, he called in sick. He's got to have his tonsils out, so I'm taking his place till he heals up. It's just a bit part, but—well, hey—I wanted to help out."

Gypsy saw behind the "cool guy" exterior to Jody's sensitive young man's heart, thrilled at the honor of "joining the company." For weeks he'd faithfully performed any humble backstage tasks thrown his way, and now he was to be rewarded.

"Why, Jode, that's just great! I'll be so proud of you!"

Jody shifted in embarrassed pleasure. "Oh, sure. I'll probably be up for the Academy Award, or whatever they give stage actors." His deprecating humor didn't fool Gypsy. She knew he appreciated her praise.

She went on into the barn to watch the rehearsal. Until this summer she'd never realized the dozens of seemingly inconsequential touches that, when put together judiciously, weave the fabric of theater magic. Ila was a good director; there was no doubt of that. She made suggestions, but left room for individual interpretations. She encouraged effective innovations and gave incisive explanations as to why something wasn't working, and always her eye was sharp for details.

Jody walked through his part well enough for a novice.

After a private coaching session with Ila, sandwiched between afternoon rehearsal and early supper, he made a surprisingly good debut that night. Ila said to Gypsy, "He's got a strong instinct for timing and delivery. I want to try out his singing voice; if it's any good, he might be the one for the part of the street-wise teenager in our last musical."

Gypsy, whose feelings toward Ila were even more mixed since the afternoon conversation with Reva, couldn't help being pleased that Jody had done so well. He needed opportunities to feel good about himself.

"Well, what do you know? A budding James Dean right in our midst," she joked lightly. "I'm glad I baked his favorite cake for an after-play treat."

Friday night: she was ready, at last, for this, the most exciting date of her life. All the while Gypsy had been dressing in her prettiest midsummer frock, a cape-sleeved cream sheer sprigged with violets, and brushing her hair into a glamorous pile atop her head, she'd debated: should she say anything to Dayt about Reva's talk? Or about Ila's uncharacteristic one-day slump into depression? Maybe the chance would come up by itself if she waited for an appropriate moment. She dashed on one more spray of her new cologne, bought especially for the occasion, and went out to the kitchen to make sure Reva was there preparing supper.

"Well, now, don't you look pretty?" Reva ventured, putting down her carrot scraper. "Who's the lucky man?"

"Dayt." Gypsy could feel the color rising from her neck to her cheeks. She hadn't breathed a word yet to anyone about the wonderful thing that was going on between her and Dayt; she hadn't dared until he overcame whatever strange reluctance it was that kept him from admitting to himself that he loved her. If *she* knew it, it was only a matter of time before *he* did.

"Reva," Gypsy said quickly, "if you've got everything under control here—"

"I have, so go sit on the porch and look pretty for your date with Dayt," Reva punned good-naturedly. "I'll have that supper whipped out in fifteen minutes."

Gypsy laughed as she went out to the porch, where players and apprentices were trooping in for their evening meal. Gypsy settled into the swing, relishing their flattering remarks about her appearance. How good it was to be on warm terms with them all, to feel in league with them instead of like a hostile outsider. The porch soon hummed with hungry diners munching their way through Reva's tasty repast. Whatever her failings, Reva was an excellent cook.

Gypsy suddenly remembered she had to phone her cousin Sheila, who had offered to use some of her vacation time to help out with the boardinghouse. Gypsy grinned to herself as she made her way across the crowded porch; the fact that Dan Wells seemed to light up every time Sheila came around had nothing to do with her sudden turn toward domesticity, of course. I might just as well tell She-She to come over next week and make several of us happy at the same time, she thought.

In the kitchen, she picked up the phone to dial and heard someone talking. That wasn't unusual. One of the necessary economies of the first-year theater enterprise was that the barn office was on the same phone line as the house.

But before she could hang up, a deep-toned voice stayed her hand. It was Dayt's.

"Get it settled," he was saying. "As I told you Monday afternoon, I'll see that everything is as fair to each of you as possible."

The other voice was Ila's. "Dayt, I can't help it, I feel somehow . . . guilty . . . about this. I don't want to push her out of her inheritance—"

Gypsy stood stunned, riveted to the phone she knew she should hang up immediately, and would have hung up under normal circumstances. But this—could it be *her* inheritance they were talking about?

"Ila," Dayt's deep voice counseled, "you've got to trust me. When he knew he wasn't going to get better he gave me power of attorney because he knew how . . . unstable . . . she is, how unlikely it was the two of you could work together amicably. He trusted me to do what's best for all concerned and I'm trying to do it."

"Oh, I know that, Dayt; I know your motives are right. But that other person, can you make *her* understand?"

"I think so, enough so she'll go along without fighting us. She doesn't have much business sense; I think I can convince her to take a reasonable cash settlement and go back to the life she knows best, instead of piddling around with property she doesn't know how to handle."

There was a long pause, during which Gypsy felt her life swirling down a whirlpool of betrayal. Then, "I leave this in your hands, Dayton. And I . . . I . . ." The words choked off in tears. "I'm so grateful for your help. I should have accepted your proposal years ago, before things got into such a muddle—"

"Ila," Dayt sounded warm and firm, "I'll always take care of you. It's time that Ila Danova had things go her way for a change. I want you to be free to take this theater project just as far as you can, with no 'off-stage' worries to distract you. If we don't do it this way, you'll never know when she's going to change her mind and throw a real monkey wrench into your plans."

Gypsy could stand no more. She slipped the phone onto its hook with nerveless hands. Every word had been a nail hammered into her soul. You fool, she smote herself, Dayton O'Rourke, the man you want to give your love, your trust, is *using* you. He's going to sign over your property, your link to all the Connors who've gone before, to the woman he really loves, whom he'll "always take care of." And you, Gypsy, are just an unstable "other person"—he and Gramps must have agreed on that—to be bought off with a "reasonable settlement." Oh, no wonder he brought up Matt Morris the other night! What a convenience to have Matt take you off his hands! And you, *fool*, thought you detected *love* in what was just plain old lust on Dayt's part? You're as naive as you were five years ago!

"Gypsy! What's the matter? You look like you've seen a ghost!"

Gypsy turned stricken eyes on Reva, unable to conceal the shock still reverberating through her system. "I . . . feel . . . a little ill, Reva—something isn't digesting—" She had to get out of here, find a place away from all these eyes and ears where she could accost the man who'd shattered her life. "I'm going up to the wooded patch behind the house to get some air. When Dayt comes . . ." She could barely utter his name without crying. ". . . tell him to come there, will you?" She started for the door, not waiting for a reply. Her legs were stone; they had to be told every step to take.

"Why . . . yes. . . ." Reva replied, mystification shadowing her tone.

Gypsy walked zombielike across the backyard and up the timber-grassed crispiness of the wooded knoll, heedless of the dangers to her high-heeled sandals and best nylons. Around her goldenrod and Queen Anne's lace massed in patches of mid-July splendor; birds wound down the day with evening twitterings, interrupted occasionally by a jay's raucous call; the steady burt-burt of crickets blended with the spicy fragrance of deep summer woodland. But all these beauties that once would have moved Gypsy's heart to thankful prayerfulness were dead to her now.

All the signs she'd thought pointed to a joyous future with the man she loved—she'd misread every one of them. It was more than she could comprehend—or *wanted* to comprehend.

She heard a powerful car rumbling up the lane; that would be Dayt. Her heart contracted, trying to protect itself from the coming storm. It wasn't real; she couldn't be facing this nightmarish pain.

She reached the crest of the knoll and stepped over it just far enough so no one could see her from the house. Before long she heard the slam of the kitchen door and she knew Dayt would be striding up the hill to find her. Blood beat through her veins in heavy surges that brought her out of her shocked anger to a state of unnatural awareness. She could hear twigs breaking under his sure, quick tread, smell the heady mixture of clean, healthy skin with its tingly after shave, feel the hardy fervor of his embrace—all long before he appeared suddenly within a few feet of her, stopping abruptly to gaze down on her.

The pain to her oversensitized nerves was unbearable. A lowering sun gleamed off his golden hair, highlighting a face and body handsome far beyond the mere physical, the magnetism of the man powered by more than outward appearance. A wild notion struck her: this must be the way the archangels looked, taller, fairer, more glowing than the mortals to whom they appeared. Except here was no good angel. Far from it.

"Gypsy!" His greeting was low, intense, pushed by feelings too strong for words.

She opened her mouth, but nothing came out. She registered the perfectly tailored suit of cream-beige linen, the immaculate white shirt and expensive blue-green striped silk tie that just matched his eyes; she saw in his hands a long florist's box. But all she could think of were his words, "I think I can convince her to take a reasonable cash settlement and go back to the life she knows best—"

"Gypsy, darling." He was face to face with her in one long stride, but she came to life and wrestled back from his attempted embrace.

"Get away from me!" she warned in a breathless rasp. "Get off my property and don't come near me again!"

If she'd struck him in the face with a club, he couldn't have been more stunned.

"Gypsy . . . Mary Catherine . . . what is it? What's wrong?"

Anger from some deep, poisoned well boiled up in her, clogging her brain with the acid of bitter betrayal. "You thought you'd use me, did you, to get what you wanted for

Ila?" She was shaking so hard in pained wrath she could hardly steady her voice. "You thought you'd sign my inheritance over to *her*?"

"What are you talking about?" he demanded, anger beginning to replace shock.

"I'll take you to court!" she raved. "You think just because you've got this power of attorney thing, you can just walk all over me! Well, we'll see! We'll see what a judge thinks of your turning *my* property over to *your* lady-love, 'reasonable settlement' or no! You aren't going to buy Ila's love with the only security I have in this world!"

Dayt's eyes blazed with something akin to fury, and the jut of his jaw was iron reinforcement to his ominously quiet words. "Mary Catherine, talk plainly. Just what is it you're accusing me of?"

"I know all about your plans to build a dormitory, expand the program, turn everything *I* inherited over to Ila as one big love-present. I *heard* you talking to her! I heard you call me unstable, heard you brag that you could shoo me out of the way, back to the life I know best! Well, I'll tell you something, Mr. Big Wheel—you not only aren't going to get by with that, *she's* not going to be here next season. If it weren't for the innocent bystanders, I'd run her off tonight!"

Even to her enraged eyes, it seemed as if Dayt suddenly grew another foot taller. He loomed over her so powerfully only her blind fury kept her from backing away. He slammed the florist's box at her feet with a force that broke it open, spilling long-stemmed red roses like splotches of blood from her riven heart.

"You eavesdropped? You—" He stopped, seeming to

rein in his tongue with superhuman effort. "That's the kind of man you think I am?"

"Aren't you?" she hissed. "Oh, I admit you warned me; all the mumble-jumble about not being God, and worrying about my soul ... and your goody-goody refusal to 'seduce' me. Take your fake Christianity and get away from me!"

Under his tan his face turned white and strained. He let her ugly depiction stand in the air until he finally found words for his pain. "So this is what's on the other side of your passion? Disbelief? Security in a bit of land? Reliance on your own suspicious mind as a moral guide? You'll never change, will you, Mary Catherine? You'll never be able to look beyond yourself, will you? Well, don't worry—I'll never come near you again!"

He spun on his heel and strode off toward the house, fierce as lightning ready to strike.

Gypsy followed him a few feet to the top of the rise, then stopped cold. "Oh, God! Oh, dear God!" The words were a plea, not a curse. She sank to her knees and her head doubled down to her thighs, so broken with angry grief was she. This was worse even than Gramps's death; this was the deliberate removal of love—even respect—and it left her bereft of everything that made her life worth living.

No tears came, only a dry, rasping breath that seared worse than fire. At length she heard Dayt's car roar off down the lane, then the incoming autos of theater-goers arriving for the evening performance. She crouched, desolate, for a long time; then she rose heavily and dragged off to her home. It, and Jody, were all she had left.

chapter

9

THE HEAT LAY IN A DEADLY, sullen blanket, oppressing the land. Gypsy and Jody sat at a porch table dawdling over their early morning breakfast on this unnaturally sultry first day of August. Tonight was Jody's big night; thanks to his successful emoting as Jimmy Tate's stand-in, he'd landed the small but meaty role of a tough teenager in *Good Sam*, the last play of the season. The original allegory revolved around the adventures of a small-town Christian wending his way through the dangerous layers of big city life, stopping to help at times when others passed by.

"Are you going to come watch me tonight?" Jody asked, using his sweating orange juice glass to form rings-within-rings on the tabletop.

"Why, of course, Jody," Gypsy answered, roused from her now-common lethargy. "I wouldn't miss it for anything. I'll be at the kiddie matinee this afternoon, too, to see your doggy act."

"Oh, that—" Jody chuckled self-consciously. "Boy, is it *hot* inside that dog outfit!" Jody and the other apprentices were performing an animal fable that tickled the children while making the point that God loves all his diverse creation. Jody drank off his juice in one long swig, as if fortifying himself against coming dehydration.

"You're learning to suffer for your art," Gypsy kidded, "and you look cute with one ear up and the other cocked sideways. Gramps would sure be surprised to see you running around in what was once his old brown blanket, plus a couple of bent coat hangers, wouldn't he?"

"Yeah, I guess so," Jody grinned. He, like Gypsy, was in the uniform of the day, cut-offs and a sleeveless knit shirt. He turned now to sit with one long leg stretched along the picnic bench, and Gypsy noticed how much he'd filled out in the past few months. Wholesome food and plenty of exercise had changed him from a gangly scarecrow to a fast developing young man. He was going to be good looking, she realized. When he went back to high school this fall, the girls were going to see him in a different light from the scrawny city kid of April. Clothes—it would take a whole new wardrobe of jeans and shirts to cover him decently for the school year. Where would she get the money?

"Well," he said, swinging both legs off the bench to sit leaning on one knee exactly the way Dayt did sometimes, "I've gotta get over to O'Rourke Farms. Reva said the grass needs mowing bad. Dayt was right; I think she *does* measure that grass with a one inch ruler!"

Gypsy's hand made a nervous sweep of her hair, drawn back into one long braid. "Oh . . . uh, I've been meaning to tell you . . . you don't need to work for Dayt any more. I mean, with your increased acting chores, and all," she finished lamely.

Jody's eyes turned on her, questioning. "Gyps," he said carefully, "I've been wondering . . . has something . . . gone wrong . . . between you and Dayt? All of a sudden he's not around here any more, and Reva doesn't help you—"

"I haven't needed Reva with Sheila on hand," Gypsy quickly explained. "And I understand Dayt has gone on vacation. That's what Reva says, anyway." She must be careful, Gypsy knew, what she told Jody about Dayt. He idolized the man; to destroy his faith in the most important male role model in his life would be a dreadful thing. Look what it had done to her to discover Dayt's true nature.

"But is that all? I thought for a while there you two might be . . . gettin' together," Jody persisted. "After that big squall at the pool, you seemed pretty soft on him until that Friday night date didn't work out."

Anguish gnawed at Gypsy's vitals, but she tried to respond calmly. "We have had a . . . disagreement. I've seen a lawyer about getting my business affairs out of Dayt's hands." She looked down at her coffee mug, unable to watch the disappointment in Jody's face. "But that doesn't mean you and Dayt can't still be friends. It's just that you don't need to work over there any more."

"Yes, I do, Gyps." He was quietly firm. "I have to live up to my agreement. And we need the money. Dayt says a real man wants to pay his own way."

What could she say? Urge him to break his word? Lie to him about their financial situation? It was precarious, to say the least. The modest fee she charged the boarders barely covered her essential expenses, and without Dayt around to sign for her, she couldn't touch a penny of Gramps's cash until the will was probated. If she followed through with her attempt to remove Dayt's power of attorney, the whole process might drag on for months, even years, or so said the lawyer she'd consulted. He wasn't optimistic. She'd have to prove to a judge that Dayt was willfully mishandling her property for the sole purpose of pleasing Ila, a fact not readily apparent to unbiased eyes if he carried through with the "reasonable cash settlement." Even if she were willing to bare her personal life in court, what could she say? That Dayt had deliberately led her on, or lied to her about the real nature of his relationship with Ila? Technically, neither was true. Try as she might, she couldn't translate, even to herself, the events of that moonlighted madness at his house into a seduction attempt on his part. It had just happened, the explosion of mutual physical attraction between them. She had recklessly dashed ahead with unfounded assumptions of his love for her. Her shoulders dropped in a gesture of defeat formerly unknown to her.

"O.K. Go ahead, Jode. Better work before the real heat sets in."

He rose in an astonishing imitation of Dayt's fluid movement. I should have known he had acting talent, Gypsy marveled, by the way he's picked up Dayt's mannerisms. He's a born mimic.

"See you for lunch," he said and ambled off to commence his duties.

Behind Gypsy the household stirred to life. She heard the pop of the toaster in the kitchen, repeated "thunks" of the refrigerator door, the more or less constant gush of water through the bathroom pipes. She stood to clear the table just as Ila emerged from the dining room, coffee cup in hand. As usual, Ila looked cool and neatly groomed, as if she were far above the mugginess that plagued everyone else with clammy sweat and touchy tempers.

"Good morning," Ila offered civilly.

Gypsy had to force herself to a polite reply. Since her discovery of the treachery afoot, the distance between her and Ila had grown from measurable to immense. True, Ila had had the decency to feel guilty about her collusion with Dayt, but it hadn't stopped her from accepting his plans.

"I was wondering, Gypsy, if we might talk out in the theater office this morning? If you can spare a few minutes?"

"What about?" Gypsy's question was sharper than she'd intended, but she could barely tolerate the woman.

Ila regarded her attentively before she replied. "For one thing, about next season."

Gypsy's head tossed before she could stop the impulse. "And what else?" she challenged grimly. She had plenty to say about "next season," but today wasn't the right time to say it.

Ila, somewhat disconcerted, said, "Jody. We have to talk about Jody."

"Now, what possible matter do we have to discuss about Jody?" Gypsy inquired icily. "Isn't he doing well? Are you afraid he'll forget his lines tonight?"

Once again Gypsy saw that flash in Ila's eyes, that momentary fire only she seemed to strike with her refusal to kowtow to the beautiful Queen Ila's wishes.

"I'd really prefer to talk privately, if you don't mind," Ila intoned with a significant nod toward the activity in the background.

Gypsy wanted to say, "Tough luck!" but she pulled herself together sufficiently to reluctantly mutter, "All right. I'll be down at the barn in a few minutes." She brushed past Ila with her collected tableware, determined to keep this meeting on her own terms as much as possible.

She deliberately fooled around fifteen minutes before she entered the barn office to confront her rival. She needed the time to counsel herself to moderation, because until she actually dislodged Dayt as her overseer, she preferred not to open this can of worms with the glamorous Ila. It wasn't revenge she sought, she told herself, but justice. Still justice with an added slap at Ila would suit her fine.

Ila, seated at her desk, glanced around the tiny cubicle that housed the business end of the theater. "Have a chair, Gypsy, if you can find one under the clutter," she half joked.

"Thanks. This'll be fine." Gypsy boldly perched right on the left corner of the desk so that Ila had to gaze up at her in her superior position.

Ila shifted slightly, her only admission of discomposure.

"Well, what is it about Jody?" Gypsy queried, carrying the ball to Ila's court.

Thoughtfully, Ila tapped a pencil against her teeth before she replied, "Something good, I think you'll agree." She leaned forward, suddenly intense. "Gypsy, Jody isn't just another boy having fun in a play."

"So?"

"So he's got immense potential. Oh, he's got a long way to go; his singing voice will require very careful training, and not before it's well past the breaking stage. But in the meantime—" She stood up, excited. "Gypsy, the boy's a sponge! He takes stage direction like no one I've worked with in years; you tell him once how to do something and he's got it! A gift like that is inborn; it can't be learned."

"I . . . realize he's talented," Gypsy said, wondering what direction this conversation was headed. "Why are you telling me this?"

Ila moved around the desk, restless. "Because I have a proposition to make and I'm not sure how you'll take it."

Gypsy, too, stood. "What kind of proposition?" A little tingle of fear threaded across her thoughts; she had an idea what was coming.

"I'd like to take Jody back with us at the end of the season, to live in Chicago and continue working with New Earth."

The fear struck home. Give up Jody? "Let me get this clear; you want to take Jody. For how long?"

"As long as he wants to stay with me. I'm not wealthy, but I can support Jody comfortably, even send him to college. Gypsy . . . ," Ila's hand touched Gypsy's arm for emphasis. "I *want* to do this for Jody!"

Gypsy jerked back, gasping at the nerve of the woman. First she'd taken Dayt, then Jesse's Barn; now she wanted Jody too? "This wouldn't be something you cooked up with your dear friend and protector, Dayton O'Rourke, would it?" she gritted through clenched teeth. "Something to make it all the easier for me to leave here, go back on the road?"

Ila searched Gypsy's angry face, apparently mystified by her reaction. "Wh—Are you thinking of doing that? Going back on the road, I mean?"

"I'm afraid not, Ila. In fact, I think I'll probably be right here long after *you're* out wondering where your easy property went. And no, I *won't* let Jody live with the kind of play-acting Christian you seem to be! I—" She stopped short; Shawn was at the door. He knocked.

"Sorry to bother you, Ila, but you said yesterday the fresnels need readjusting on downstage right?"

"Oh . . . yes, Shawn," Ila fluttered, for once not quite in command of a situation. "I'll be out in a minute. Gypsy . . ." She turned worried eyes on the girl beside her. "I have to finish this with you. What is it that makes you so hostile to me?"

"Go work on your lighting, Ila. Enjoy this theater while you can." Gypsy flipped out of the room, unable to bear the sight of the woman who seemed to have everything.

Halfway to the house, Gypsy came to an abrupt halt; a bright red foreign car, a roadster, was easing into the drive, purring to a throaty stop. "Matt!" In the turmoil of the past days, she'd forgotten her former employer's intent to see her.

"Gypsy-girl, you're looking great!" Fit, tan Matt Morris slid sunglasses to rest atop his dark curls and hoisted his lithe frame to the ledge behind the cushions of his jaunty two-seater.

"Why Matt, so are you." His expensive tan cottons, her faded grubbies—the contrast embarrassed her.

He hopped to the ground and came to take her hand.

"I like your car," she commented politely. Anyone who drove a car like that wanted it mentioned.

"Do you? It's a '68 Austin-Healey 3000, the last of its line. Makes a good buggy for tooling around country roads."

He hasn't changed, Gypsy reflected. Matt liked to surround himself with desired things, then treat them as casual amusements, which, of course, emphasized rather than underplayed his acquisitions. It was the quality Gypsy least liked in his otherwise attractive personality.

Matt looked at her closely, genuinely sympathetic. "I'm sorry about your grandfather, Gypsy. I was out of the country when—he—"

"Yes. I understand, Matt. I'm . . . uh . . . I'm getting over it," she murmured.

"That's good. Things should only be the best for you, Gyps."

"Oh . . . thanks."

"Which is why I'm here with an idea I think would be *very* good for you—"

Gypsy responded quickly, "If it's about my going on the circuit—"

"Better than that. Much better." His eyes crinkled; he was apparently much pleased with what he was about to offer.

"Oh?" What could he—?

"Can we talk?" he asked, glancing around for a likely conversation spot.

"Oh . . . sure!" Gypsy flustered, remembering her manners. "On the porch; I'll get us some iced tea."

Over the cold drinks, Matt revealed, by degrees, his reason for coming to see Gypsy. "The countryside in this area is beautiful, isn't it, Gypsy? Hills, trees—very much like the English Cotswolds."

"I haven't seen them—"

"Take my word for it. They're charm with a capital C."

"Oh." What was he working up to? Matt seldom engaged in idle chitchat.

"Yes, ever since the O'Rourkes had me down for their anniversary party, I've had an idea rattling around the back of my mind." He observed the rim of his glass, a

177

speculative smile tugging the corner of his mouth. "How many Chicagoans, do you suppose, long for an occasional vacation—even a few days—in a simple pastoral setting? A place where they can enjoy—even *wallow*—in the glories of nature and still be waited on hand and foot, of course!"

"Why ...," Gypsy shared a chuckle at his ironic depiction of the armchair ruralist. "I suppose ... quite a few?"

"Hundreds. Thousands. And I know right where they could find such a place—for a healthy fee, naturally...." He let the sentence dangle enticingly.

Now she caught his drift. "You mean ... here? This place?"

He leaned forward, enthusiastic as only an entrepreneur can be at the scent of a new project. "Gyps, I'm talking a country inn, riding trails, a swimming pool, health spa—you name it, we'll have it! I've looked into this, Gypsy, and I've seen farms with less to offer than this one turned into mighty profitable resorts."

"Wait! Wait!" she cried, breath-stricken. "You're going a little fast for me! I *won't* sell this land—"

"You don't have to. That's the beauty of it. You give me a long lease; I provide the capital and planning; and you, Gypsy—" He took her hand. In his gaze was something beyond friendship. "*You* preside."

"Preside?" she questioned, tentative.

"You'll be the ... lady ... of the place. The overseer who never lifts a finger for drudgery; you'll manage the resort, play the piano, and look beautiful; you'll make every person who comes here happier for having known you. As I am."

Gypsy's eyes fell before the frank tenderness in his gaze. Oh, dear, she fretted, like everything else in my life, this is going to be complicated.

"It . . . it's an intriguing idea—" she stammered.

"And one that will make you wealthy." The faint crack in his voice that had betrayed the deep feeling in his previous statement was gone. "I'll see to it that your share of the profit is generous, *very* generous."

"But I already have a theater going—"

"Keep it. Or not. Whichever you choose. Keep this house, if you want. We can build the inn farther back in the woods." Little things didn't deter Matt from his purpose.

"There's one other factor, Matt. My . . . uh . . . my grandfather gave Dayton O'Rourke power of attorney over my affairs until he 'deems me capable' of running them myself."

"So? Dayt's a good businessman; he'll see the sense of my idea," he countered, sure of his own financial acumen.

"Uh . . . I . . . don't think so," Gypsy hedged. "We've had a disagreement, a serious one, and . . . Oh, well, I might as well tell you, Matt," she blurted. "I've seen a lawyer about getting out of Dayt's control, and he says it's not that easy."

Matt didn't say anything for a minute. She saw doubt, annoyance, and determination pass in rapid succession across his handsome features. "Gyps," he said at last, "I think highly of Dayton O'Rourke; he's a fine lawyer. But so are mine. And they're used to getting me what I want. You say the word, and I'll get you free of Dayton O'Rourke."

So there it was, right in her lap: the solution to her

financial problems. And best of all, the chance for justice, with a tremendous added slap at both Ila and . . . and. . . . Even in her heart, she couldn't say his name.

"I'll have to think, Matt. Give me some time?"

"Sure, Gyps. All the time you need."

chapter

10

THE HEAT WAS TERRIBLE. At lunch everyone picked at the food, making Gypsy wish she'd forgotten the whole meal. Her quarrel with Ila, her plot to use Matt to wreak revenge—might as well call it by its true name—sat like wounds on her mind. In spite of her intemperate words to Ila, she began to debate herself. Did she have the right to deny Jody his chance in the theater? No matter what she thought of Ila, the woman knew her business. From her own experience, she knew that a professional artist needs to start early and use every opportunity that came by; in a small town like Sauk Valley, acting experience would be severely limited.

Of course, if she did go along with Matt's plan, wouldn't she have enough money to send him off to a good school, maybe one that specialized in drama? But there was a drawback to going in with Matt: he plainly wanted their relationship to be more than business. What if he asked her to marry him? Any liaison without matrimony was out as far as she was concerned, but what if he *did* propose? Would he think she was "reneging" somehow when she refused? Because as far as she could see into the future, there would be no other man in her life. Not after Dayt.

Oh, Gypsy moaned inwardly, how did I ever get into this no-win position?

It was probably just happenstance, but at lunchtime, Jody brought his lightly filled plate to sit by Ila, who kept watching Gypsy with her big, questioning eyes. Would she dare mention her plan to Jody in spite of Gypsy's objection? She and Jody were chatting about the night's performance, Jody understandably excited.

"You know, when Gypsy told me we were goin' to move to a little farm in Illinois, near Peoria yet, I thought, What in the world will I do there? I thought maybe I'd be milkin' cows and stuff, you know, like they do on T.V. farms. I never dreamed I'd be up on a stage! With a bunch of Christians, yet!"

Ila laughed, and even Gypsy, pouring iced tea at the next table, had to smile briefly at his inelegant but honest confession.

"Is being with a 'bunch of Christians' such a bad experience, Jody?" Ila asked. "Have you discovered any of us to have two heads or a stake through the heart?"

Jody laughed his rough, boyish chortle, then said soberly, "Uh-uh. If you and Dayt and Gypsy, and all these other guys," he said, indicating the other diners, "are Christians . . . I mean . . . I thought maybe there'd be a lot of preachin' or strict rules, but you guys . . . you guys. . . ."

Gypsy turned around; she saw a deep flush come up over Jody's face as he stumbled into an emotional situation he hadn't counted on. His next words were so soft no one but Gypsy and Ila heard them. "You're the best people I've ever known. If you guys are Christians—well, do you think . . . maybe someday. . . could I be one, too?"

Over Jody's head, Gypsy and Ila locked eyes in realization that this was a decisive moment—perhaps the *most* important moment—in the boy's young life. Gypsy's heart quivered with a fearful shock; what would happen when Jody found out the real nature of the three very weak, very flawed individuals he now looked to for spiritual guidance?

"That's a serious decision to make, Jody," Ila said quietly, "the most important of your life. You will need to pray and talk with those who can help you understand the step you're taking. Then if you still want to make that commitment, we'll all be happy to help you become a Christian."

Ila's arm came around Jody for a quick hug and Gypsy touched his cheek, her eyes misted with love and concern for his salvation. Indeed, for her own. The doubting, resentful cloud that hung between her and the Lord shadowed more and more heavily over her thoughts. How was she fit to guide Jody?

Jody, flustered, jumped up from the table. "Hey, I better find my dog suit—" He turned first to Ila, then Gypsy. "But I mean what I said. You two'll help me, won't you, with the counseling stuff?" It was obviously difficult for him to handle a subject so close to his heart.

"Of course," Ila assured him.

"Yes, Jode," Gypsy answered hesitantly. As he left the table, she and Ila again exchanged glances. I've got to work out some kind of truce with her before our quarrel jeopardizes that boy's soul, Gypsy told herself. Somehow . . . Somehow . . .

The others were moving around, leaving half-finished lunches to get ready for the matinee. Gypsy started to speak to Ila, but the director was already in the midst of two or three minor problems that had to be solved before two o'clock.

Sheila, who was supposed to be Gypsy's helper, got up from beside Dan, where she'd taken her lunch, to follow him out to the barn. She makes a better love-sick calf than assistant, Gypsy thought wryly. Oh well. She supervised the table clearing and dishwashing, then wandered down to the barn. The first busload of children had arrived and were happily indulging in their peanut-butter-sandwich-and-Kool-Aid lunches. Uncle Worth, correctly assuming that some theater-goers would want to bring lunches with them, had built several sturdy bench-tables to set in the catalpa grove behind the barn; it made a good place for not only those who wanted to picnic, but also for children who needed to frolic off some excess energy before show-time.

Gypsy sat on the back doorstep of the barn to watch the antics of the present group. They ranged in age from preschool to perhaps fifth grade, a colorful assortment of sun-suited and shorts-clad moppets seemingly unaffected by the steamy weather. Only their hard-pressed chaperones looked ready to wilt as they rode herd over the rambunctious sprites.

I wonder what our children would have been like? Gypsy allowed the forbidden thought to enter once more into her consciousness. From the moment Dayt had teased her that maybe she needed a "few good babies," and put her so gently into his bed, an imaginary child had lain nestled in her heart, the child of their love, who would someday in reality lie at her nourishing breast. Longing sweet and terrible in its futility swept her now, clouding her eyes with tears for what might have happened. Unfortunately, it had only been *her* dream, hadn't it?

She sighed, a long, headachy exhalation that brought no relief. Matt's plan revolved around her brain in a crazy match with Ila's scheme to get Jody from her; over the battle brooded her conscience, which knew clear as a bell that whoever said revenge is sweet wasn't thinking about its possible effects on innocent bystanders. Like Jody.

Gypsy sat facing west; off to the south, heat lightning flickered around the edges of dirty gray clouds that had lowered there since morning. The whole sky had a brassy look to it that foreboded rain, possibly a storm, before nightfall. If this were spring, Gypsy mused, I'd say this was tornado weather. But I never heard of one around here in August.

Jody plopped down beside her, dog suit in hand. "Gyps, the zipper won't work. Can you fix it?"

She examined the concealed back zipper. "Mmm. Got a bit of cloth caught in it." She began to work the material out of the zipper teeth. "Wow! I'm glad you're the one wearing this thing today!" she exclaimed, sweating under the weight of the heavy cloth on her lap.

"Yeah," Jody agreed. "But it's kinda worth it. You know, to hear the kids laugh. I can't wait till next summer. Rehearsal and performance—even stage crew—it doesn't seem like work to me, Gyps."

Gypsy had the zipper worked almost free, but her hands fell still. Next summer—he was assuming there'd be a Jesse's Barn playhouse. He didn't even know he had an opportunity to act all winter, to study his craft with the talented Ila.

"You . . . you really care about theater life, don't you, Jode?" she quavered.

"Oh, yeah, Gyps. I know what I want to be: an actor in Christian theater. Even if I mess up tonight, I'm goin' to stick with it. See," he said, his voice breaking a little in its adolescent urgency, "it's like you and your keyboards. I've watched you; you always sit still just a minute before you start playin', then you take someone else's notes and you make a song. And you never play anything exactly the same way twice, so it's *your* song even if someone else wrote the notes. That's the way I feel about actin'; I get to take someone else's words and then the way I say 'em, the way I act 'em, that makes 'em *my* character. Neat, huh?"

"Yes. That's . . . neat." Gypsy's heart turned over. She had to tell Jody about Ila's offer even though it would probably take him away from her now when she needed him just as much as he'd ever needed her. Her doubts about Ila's fitness as a guardian—was Ila any worse in her tricky selfishness than Gypsy was in her lack of faith?

"Jode," she. began slowly, turning back to the zipper problem, "How did you like going to Sauk Valley High this spring?"

He looked at her, surprised. "Well, okay. It was a lot different from Thomas Jefferson Junior High in New York City, but it was okay. Why? What's that got to do with anything?"

"Well, how would you like to go to a big school again? In Chicago? And work with the New Earthers year round?"

Jody's eyes lighted. "Gyps, are we movin' to Chicago?"

She fumbled at the zipper, trying hard to force out what

must be spoken. "Not 'we,' Jody. Just you. Ila wants you to come live with her so that you can get the acting training you need. You don't have to go," she quickly added. "It's up to you."

Jody didn't respond. In his clear, young eyes Gypsy saw the conflict building. "But I can't leave you here alone," he said at last. "Like Dayt says, it's not safe for you to live alone in the country."

"Jode, you musn't worry about me. I'm ... uh ... thinking of going on the road again, at least for this winter," she fibbed. "You have to do what will develop your talents—"

"Like you did when you took me in? Or when you came home to be with your grandpa? That really did a lot for your musical career, Gyps!" Jody's sarcasm was gentle.

"That was different."

"Why?"

"Because . . ." she stopped, then grinned ruefully. "Because I did it. Don't you be like me. You take the opportunity to really study your craft so you don't end up a half-baked artist who can't even tell what key you're playing in."

The heavy rumble of two more buses arriving cut across her words.

"Oh, hey, I gotta get into my costume," Jody said, scrambling up. "Thanks for fixin' the zipper, Gyps. I'll talk to you later about goin' with Ila." He loped into the men's dressing room.

Gypsy got to her feet. At least he's not going to leave me without *some* regrets, she thought. I guess I ought to be grateful for that.

Another deep growling took her attention, but this wasn't a bus. Thank heavens! Three busloads of children would fill the little theater to capacity. No, this was thunder bellowing around the now-roiling clouds off in the southwest. Good thing it was close to "curtain time." The audience would be safely under cover before the rain got here.

Gypsy mopped at her steaming forehead. She closed the bottom half of the back door so that the half-pint crowd would enter through the front gate. The admission charge wasn't high at Jesse's Barn, but it was definitely essential to the carrying out of the operation.

Gypsy helped the little ones, now piling in ahead of their harried sponsors, to settle in seats close to their friends, find the much-needed restrooms, get a drink from the step-up fountain—all the emergencies common to an audience of tots. She was standing back by the office when the play began and the warm-suited "animals" came capering forth to delight the small fry.

"Gypsy?" Ila beckoned from the office door. "Please, we have to talk!" she whispered.

Reluctantly, Gypsy followed her into the stifling cubicle. They had to shut the door to avoid disturbing the players.

"Gypsy, I have to know something." Ila's lowered voice was strained. "What did you mean about me being a 'play-acting Christian'? And losing my 'easy property'? Has Dayt told you something I don't know?"

Gypsy stared at her. "Dayt hasn't told me anything; I found out about your scheme all on my own."

"My 'scheme'? I don't understand what you're talking about. I have many plans, but I don't consider any of them 'schemes.'"

"I don't suppose you do, Ila. I suppose you've convinced yourself that anything that conveys the Christian message as effectively as New Earth justifies whatever means are used to support it."

"I certainly have *not!*" the titian-haired Ila protested. "What *is* it you think I've done? I won't live with the name 'hypocrite.'"

A rolling boom of thunder reverberated through the barn, jiggling the plywood office walls.

"What *do* you call someone who talks about Christ, then pushes another out of her own property, all through the oh-so-legal device of 'power of attorney'?"

"But I—"

"For Jody's sake, I want to give you and Dayt a chance to back off before I have to go to court to fight you, Ila. I don't want Jody to know at this point just how false some Christian faces can be."

Ila went milk-white. "I didn't push her out of her property! There was no other way to handle it, none at all! And why are *you* going to fight us?"

Gypsy's temper soared. "Who's this 'her' you're talking about? *I'm* the one who's inheriting Jesse's Barn and the acreage around it! It's *my* property Dayt's going to buy up and give to you!"

Ila stared at Gypsy as if the younger woman had lost her mind. "Where in the world did you ever get that idea?"

The instant, bitter remembrance of that vile phone conversation trashed the last of Gypsy's restraint. "From your own mouth," she ground out. "I heard you and Dayt talking about the 'unstable one'—*me*—and how he was going to use his legal power to make you all safe and cozy here, secure from *my* erratic behavior!"

A tremendous burst of thunder roared over them, and the wind picked up. Then rain commenced a violent tattoo against the barn.

Enlightenment swept Ila's face. "Sit down," she commanded softly. "You and I have a terrible misunderstanding to clear up."

Against her will, Gypsy sat. For Jody's sake, she kept telling herself, for Jody's sake do everything you can to resolve this peaceably. Don't disillusion him the way Dayt and Ila have you.

"Yes?" she muttered.

Ila's voice was barely audible above the driving rain. "I knew someone came onto the line the last time I called Dayton; I never dreamed it was *you* listening in, but—" She waved down Gypsy's protest. "since you did, let me tell you what you really heard. Your grandfather wasn't the only man to give Dayton power of attorney. So did my husband before he became too ill to think any more."

"Your—*what*?" Gypsy jerked forward, astounded. No one had ever mentioned a Mr. Danova.

Ila held up her left hand; the emerald studded gold band spoke its true significance. "My husband," she repeated. The same lines of dejection Gypsy had seen in her once before sloped Ila's usually firm shoulders. "Have you ever heard of Alzheimer's disease?"

"Why . . . yes," Gypsy stuttered, "everyone has heard of it—" The unhappy darkening of Ila's expressive eyes stilled further words.

"My husband is fifty years old; he's a helpless invalid."

"Oh . . . Ila!" Gypsy's heart, always as quick to sympathize as to condemn, filled with compassion. "I didn't know . . . I didn't realize—"

"Maybe I should have told you, Gypsy, but I'm still in the process of accepting it. I can't talk about it easily."

Ila rose, turning her back to Gypsy. "One day I was the woman who had everything: good looks, good health, good career, and a husband I adored. The next—I can't tell you what it means to see someone you love slip away day by day into the darkness. A bright mind—destroyed. He's in a nursing home now; he needs constant care. That's where I go every other Sunday." She turned to face Gypsy. "It's funny; the doctors say there's no hope, nothing they can do, but I keep praying. Maybe someday, before it's too late, a miracle will happen and I'll have my Tony back. As it is, I live for the rare moments when he seems to recognize me. They're priceless to me."

Gypsy, trembling, got to her feet. "Ila, can you ever forgive me? I thought . . . I didn't know—"

"I specifically asked Dayton not to tell anybody down here about Tony. I'm just not strong enough yet to answer questions, to be pitied. But still, I don't understand how you could have thought Dayton O'Rourke could be a party to anything underhanded. The man's integrity itself."

Gypsy struggled to meet Ila's eyes. "It just sounded so bad—I was so wrapped up in myself—"

"When I married Tony eight years ago, he was a widower with one grown daughter, Christine. That's who you heard Dayton and me discussing. She's a . . . social butterfly sort of person, more interested in hard cash than in investment. Dayton advised me some time ago to buy out Christine's shares in her father's enterprises. I refused, not wanting her to feel I was shoving her out of her father's life. Unfortunately, Dayton was right. Christine and I simply can't run Tony's financial affairs together."

"Then . . . she's the . . . unstable one?"

"Yes."

Gypsy sat, head bowed, and the rain overhead thundered down with less force than the guilty remorse pounding through her soul. Wrong. She had been so wrong in her ugly suspicions. No wonder Dayt despised her. She felt a gentle hand on her shoulder.

"Are you in love with Dayton, Gypsy?"

Gypsy slowly raised her tormented violet eyes to the older woman's emerald ones. There was no need to answer.

"And you thought Dayton was in love with me?"

Gypsy nodded a mute yes.

Ila's smile was friendly but sad. "Maybe when I was his twenty-three-year-old speech teacher, and he was my seventeen-year-old-star debater—I coached debate in those days—maybe he had a crush on me. Boys do get them on 'older women,' you know, but that passed long ago. Now, out of all my friends, most of whom are Christians, Dayton's one of the few who never seems to doubt that Tony is still a person and that I still love him, even if he's no longer the strong, capable man I married." She shook her head. "You'd be surprised how many have advised me to divorce him, marry again while I'm still young enough to have the children I've always wanted. Not Dayton. He understands love. And loyalty."

Gypsy sat silent; what could she say?

"If you're going to love Dayton, you'd better accept right now that he'll always be concerned about his brothers and sisters. He came back into my life when we were both hurting—he over an early-youth love affair that just went on and on because he felt conscience bound to continue to the point when the woman walked out and I over my dear Tony. But he put aside his troubles to guide me through the worst days of my life."

Gypsy's mind and heart churned, partly with a strange and silly relief that Ila hadn't been the woman Dayt had been involved with. Somehow, not knowing the woman made it easier to forgive, as God had done already. Mostly, though, she worried about what Dayt thought of her. To him she must seem immensely disloyal, totally incapable of Ila's kind of unconditional love. Her rash, jealous nature—what a shambles it had made of her life. "Ila," she stammered, laying aside the foolish pride that had cut her off from this brave woman's friendship, "I need . . . I need help, from God, from someone who can show me how to put my life under his control. Will you—?"

Ila's reply was forestalled by a crash that sent both women rushing to the window. A bolt of lightning had struck the electric power transformer some few feet from the barn. A wave of startled murmurs rose from the audience on the other side of the office door. Gypsy and Ila dashed out into the theater where, of course, the stage lights were out and Mark had swiftly risen to announce, "Stay calm, everybody. See, the rain is letting up. We'll call the light company and have that transformer fixed in a jiffy. In the meantime, our play will go on."

Outside the wind and rain had abated, but it was an unnatural calm. A yellowish-green light tinted everything sickly, and the air seemed hard to breathe. Just as the players resumed their story, a tinkle, then a fierce rattle bombarded the roof; within seconds windows were smashing under the onslaught of golf-ball-sized hailstones.

"Take cover!" Gypsy yelled; over the shrieks of the children, the adults began a quick evacuation of the little ones from the tiered chairs to safer shelter under the two sets of wooden risers. Those who couldn't cram under there huddled under chairs on the floor row or pressed tight to the solid ends of the concrete risers.

Gypsy, hovering protectively over a half-dozen scared youngsters jammed flat against one such abutment, heard a roar off in the distance which she first thought was sustained thunder. But it drew steadily nearer, its volume increasing in direct proportion to the rapid disappearance of light. Then she knew!

"It's a tornado!" she cried. "Everybody down! Pull up your knees! Cover your heads with your arms!"

The roar was earsplitting, the barn interior black as pitch. Gypsy fell over the children crouching near her, stretching her arms to protect as many as possible.

Suffocating lack of air! Pressure bursting against the walls of her brain! Shattering explosions, debris whirling, dust filling her lungs! Terror too great for words—and over it all, a great, inundating tide of love—for the little children, for the New Earthers, for Uncle Worth and all his brood and Gram and Gramps and mother and father. For Jody and Dayt—all the people she'd ever loved. They stood clear before her mind's eye; behind them radiated a light and warmth that opened her lips. "Jesus! Dear Jesus! Be with us now! All of us!"

Then it was over. For only a few seconds, nature had laid a devastating hand on her children and taught them the true fragility of their physical existence. Gypsy, not sure she was still alive, stirred, lifting herself off the children half-squashed under her. All around were moans, whimperings, whispered exclamations as the occupants of Jesse's Barn crawled to their feet. Torrential rain slashed through the west corner of the roof, where a jagged hole gaped to the sky, but unbelievably, miraculously, the rest of the building was intact! The tornado, exercising its distinctive fickleness, had spared Jesse's Barn!

While chaperones hurriedly began collecting their charges, Gypsy and the New Earthers moved from group to group, checking superficial wounds, comforting, assuring the children and themselves that the worst was over and that they were all in God's hands. Fortunately, the risers had caught most of the glass and other debris.

Then a fact hit Gypsy: Jody was nowhere around. "Mark, have you seen Jody?" she inquired anxiously.

"No, Gyps. Here, help me get a bandage on this little fellow's arm. He's got a long scratch and the blood's scaring him."

Gypsy soothed the child while Mark got gauze from the first-aid kit, but over the boy's head she scanned worriedly for Jody. Repeated inquiries of all the players who came by yielded the same answer: "I haven't seen him."

Then Theresa remembered something. "Say, right before that bolt of lightning struck, he was rummaging in the costumes looking for that raincoat we use in *Good Sam*. Said he needed it because he'd forgotten a prop up at the house for the last scene of the matinee. You don't suppose—he wouldn't be crazy enough to dash up there in this storm, would he?" she gasped, round-eyed.

Gypsy's heart plummeted. Yes, he was enamored enough of acting to do just such a stunt. "Theresa, take this little boy, please!" she commanded, and ran to the main entrance. The rain was a driving current; she tore out into it, heedless of the voices behind her warning her to wait. She struggled toward the house, straining for a glimpse of it. Closer and closer she came, but the outlines of it evaded her. Then she saw: the house was no more!

"Jody! Jody!" she screamed repeatedly. The rain filled her mouth, but she kept calling as she clambered up onto what was left of the first floor—the floor itself. "Jody!" She groped forward, stopping right where the beige and brown linoleumed kitchen floor used to be. It was caved in; she could see down into the laundry area of the basement. What was that protruding from a pile of destruction between the clothes dryer and the wall? A dog's ear, crazily flopped across a broken board!

An eerie creaking overhead jerked Gypsy's eyes upward. The big oak tree that had stood guard over the back porch ever since the house was built yawned forward, split by the storm. If it fell before she got Jody out of the basement—

Gypsy leaped for the basement steps, wiping rain from her eyes as she dodged debris, half falling in her haste to dig out Jody. Her mind held one continuous prayer: *please, God, help Jody!* She tugged wildly at a board jammed over the ridiculous dog ear, oblivious to the splinters gouging into her palms.

"Watch out, Gypsy! I'll get him out." Two powerful hands pulled her back, and she looked up to see Dayt's rain-soaked but determined face above hers. She nearly fainted with relief.

chapter
11

It was just after dawn; Gypsy was aware of that when she wakened, bent face down on the hospital bed beside which she'd sat all night holding Jody's hand. Her eyes focused on that big-jointed boy's hand still resting under her protective clasp. He was safe! Thanks to God, he was safe!

"Gypsy, dear? Can you sit up?" It was Aunt May's soft voice and Uncle Worth's solid strength helping her to an upright position. Jody was deep in sleep.

"Oh, how long—" Gypsy mumbled, easing back into her chair. Every muscle in her body ached. Uncle Worth began gently massaging her neck and upper back.

"We brought you some of Sheila's clothes, dearie," Aunt May whispered close to her ear. "Uncle Worth is going down to the cafeteria to get you some breakfast while you take a nice refreshing shower and slip into something clean. We'd have been here sooner, but, oh, there were so many to be looked after!"

"Your home—?" Gypsy whispered, alarmed.

"Not a stick disturbed," Uncle Worth assured her. "But a lot of folks weren't so lucky. We've opened up Jesse's Barn to those who've no roof over their head today. Knew you'd think that was the thing to do."

"Of course!" Gypsy agreed without a quibble. "Was anybody killed?"

"No, praise the Lord!" Aunt May replied.

"Lots of injuries, but most people were as fortunate as the boy here, nothing critical," Uncle Worth added. "Jody was mighty lucky to fall through the kitchen floor where he did. If he hadn't landed between the wall and the clothes dryer, the falling debris might have given him far more than a mild concussion. And, of course, being a limber thirteen-year-old probably saved him from broken bones."

Gypsy nodded her agreement, still too shaken by Jody's near-miss to talk about it without choking up.

"And . . . and O'Rourke Farms? Was it damaged?" she asked. Dayt had hurried right back to rescue work once he'd deposited Jody at the hospital in Shawana and learned he'd be all right.

"A machine shed blew away but both houses were spared. 'Course Dayt and the Thompsons have opened their doors and their pantries to everybody who can crowd in. Reva's been cooking nonstop since last night, she says, on that old gas stove in her basement she uses for canning," Aunt May confided in her usual conspiratorial tones. "Now, Worth, you run along and get Gypsy some food and then we've got to get back to Sauk Valley. Everyone who's able is out picking up whatever belongings they can find and trying to return them to the rightful owners. The New Earthers have been just wonderful that way. For one thing, they're searching the surrounding area for anything of yours they can recover, dear."

"That's good of them," Gypsy said, "but as long as we're all here, and Jody's going to be all right—" She ended with a gesture that said, What more could we ask?

"That's right, Gyps. And you know you and Jody are to come live at our house," Uncle Worth said as he left for the cafeteria. "There'll always be room."

"Thank you, Uncle Worth," Gypsy murmured, tears springing to her eyes at her uncle's generosity.

Later, when she'd showered and got into Sheila's soft-green cotton jumpsuit (a bit large for her, but at least decent), her relatives left her sitting at Jody's bedside consuming the welcome breakfast Uncle Worth had brought up to her. Jody still slumbered peacefully, but she wanted to be right there when he first woke up.

She relived the harried scene of yesterday's rescue when Dayt had got Jody uncovered, and, with Shawn's help, out of the basement moments before the split oak tree crashed over the remains of the house. They'd loaded Jody into the back of Dayt's pickup and tied a tarpaulin over it to protect Jody and Gypsy from the rain. With all the telephones out for miles around, there'd been no possibility of calling an ambulance. Then the slow ride through driving rain, dodging fallen trees and other storm wreckage, to the hospital. Before they'd got there, Jody had come to his understandably groggy senses. Tests showed nothing more serious than a light concussion and numerous cuts and bruises, but it was considered necessary to keep him at least overnight for further observation.

Gypsy sipped her coffee and watched over her ward. Oh, how young and vulnerable he looked against the pillow, forehead patched with gauze and a neat bit of sewing where his chin had been torn open.

Love, deep and unlimited, welled in her. He was such a special boy, talented and strong. God wanted this boy for his service, she was sure of that, and already Jody was feeling his call. But how could he best be prepared to answer? By staying with her? Or by going with Ila?

One word from me, one indication of how much I need him, and he'll feel duty-bound to stay with me, she thought. But is that what God wants?

And where do *I* go from here? she wondered. It was as if she'd had to lose everything. First Gramps, then Dayt, Jody, her very home. And Jesse's Barn. In the long hours of the past night, she'd come to one decision: Matt Morris's proposed resort was not for her. Revenge had a bitter flavor she intended never again to taste, and as to running a business empire, even a tiny one sponsored by a good friend who'd like to be the love in her life, that wasn't her style.

No, she'd sell her land to Dayt because he'd preserve and improve it. And the barn? To her, it was a beloved bit of family history, but to Ila, it was partial recompense for a life bereft of so much. In keeping with Gramps's wish that the barn be used for the Lord's work, what better could Gypsy do with it than to make it a gift outright to Ila?

But what course was Gypsy to take with Jody? Why couldn't she see a clear answer?

A middle-aged nurse, all efficiency, rustled in to check the elderly man behind the divider curtain of the two-bed room. He was hard of hearing, and between the nurse's shouted questions and his equally loud answers, not only did Gypsy learn more than she really wanted to know about the poor old man's condition, but Jody was roused to wakefulness.

Gypsy set aside her tray and leaned forward to take his hand. "Good morning, Jody," she whispered, smiling.

It took a second for the confusion to leave his eyes.

"How's the old bean?" She nodded toward his head.

He twisted his head gingerly. "Ouch! It's still there, I can tell! Guess that's lucky, isn't it, Gyps? A little headache's nothin' compared to no head!"

Gypsy chuckled, but she couldn't speak over the lump in her throat.

Jody's gaze sobered. "You sat there all night, didn't you, Gypsy? Holdin' on to my hand. Like you did with my mom that—last day—" He swung his face toward the wall, grimacing with pain, but not before she saw the tears spring into his eyes.

"Jody . . . I. . . ." This was the first time in months his resilient front had broken to reveal his aching sense of loss. It was so unexpected Gypsy was without words.

One palm made a hurried brush to clear his eyes. "I'm never gonna forget what you did for me . . . and Mom." He turned back to her. "Not ever."

"Oh, Jody, honey. . . ." Gypsy was half out of her chair, intent upon assuring him of his place in her heart, but the nurse picked that moment to come around the curtain. Instantly Jody resumed his usual spunky air.

"Well, it's good to see you're awake and alert, Mr. Harris. Let's get your temp." Over the temperature and pulse-taking ritual, the nurse remarked casually, "Miss Johnson will be in in a few minutes to give you your bath."

"Huh?" The thermometer dropped from Jody's alarmed mouth. Gypsy had to turn her head to snicker at the comic relief of his horror.

"Your bath. Doctor won't make rounds before ten o'clock and you can't get out of bed before he sees you. Don't worry," she added, snapping the thermometer into its computerized holder and recording the results on a pad, "she'll let you do most of it yourself. Have a good day." She gave his arm a brisk pat and sailed out of the room.

"Gypsy! I'm not gonna let a nurse—"

Gypsy evaded his protest. "Jode, I think I'll move around a little and get the kinks out of my system while the early morning hospital routine takes place. Just behave like a gentleman and remember, the nurses are doing what will make you get better. See you in a little while, hon."

She left the room, better for the brief respite brought by humor. Surely laughter was one of God's finest gifts to the human race. No wonder Jody loved to provoke the children's mirth.

The hospital was extraordinarily busy as a result of the tornado, which had cut a swath across the entire county. Gypsy stopped here and there for words with those like herself who watched over some loved one who'd fallen victim to the storm. That there had been no fatalities was generally conceded to be miraculous. Property damage had been heavy. Lined faces and tired smiles bespoke the strain of the past sixteen hours.

Gypsy made her way to the small nondenominational chapel tucked away on the top floor. Life seemed so uncomplicated within hospital walls where others made all the decisions of vast import; but outside waited a multitude of problems for a young woman with no permanent job, no home of her own, and not one personal possession except the clothes she'd worn into the hospital yesterday.

Even her purse with her billfold, driver's license, and other identification was gone.

If ever I needed divine guidance, it's now, Gypsy thought. She had the chapel to herself at this early hour. She slid into a smooth wooden pew and closed her eyes. For a while images of yesterday's terror burned behind them; she made no effort to fight the jumbled scenes. They had to have their hour if she were to get them back into proper perspective.

Then a sadness, profound and unspeakable, overwhelmed her. The home, the warm, loving nest of her youth where she'd always found refuge, was gone, utterly destroyed. A thousand happy moments lived there crowded on her heart: the good times with Grandma and Gramps; the hours at her piano; the lazy dreaming in the porch swing on rainy summer afternoons; even this hectic season with the New Earthers. She felt as if part of her living flesh had been torn away.

And where do I go from here? The question beat at her brain until she leaned forward, resting her tormented head against the frame of the seat ahead. It wasn't financial woes racking her; within weeks she could be back at her former profession making a living. And, of course, eventually she'd have a little something from Gramps's estate.

But the center of her life had never been things; it had been people. And one more than any other: Dayton O'Rourke.

So what had she done to the love he might have been discovering for her? Killed it with a full exhibition of her spiritual poverty; told him point-blank that ownership—of her property—of *him*—was her idea of security! Now, by her own hand, she was cast adrift from the one man whose love and respect meant the world to her.

Where do I go from here? Gypsy was confused, sad. Yet not desolate. Yesterday when the storm had struck, when she might have been living her last earthly moments, her heart had known where to turn; she knew the Source of the love that had filled her, lifted her above groveling fear for herself and spread her arms over the children, sent her searching for Jody, kept her by his bedside all night long praying, praying, praying. She, who had doubted God's love, understood in that moment that the unquestioning, unconditional, totally forgiving love she felt for all she knew was the embodiment of her Father's caring for all his children.

As she sat bowed and earnestly listening for God's guidance, words and phrases, then whole passages from Scripture began to filter into her tired mind. The Lord, my Rock . . . Love one another, even as I have loved you . . . Do not let your thoughts be troubled . . . Trust in God; trust also in me . . . Take no thought, saying "What shall we eat?" or "What shall we drink?" or "Wherewithal shall we be clothed?" . . . But seek ye first the kingdom of God and His righteousness and all these things shall be added unto you. . . .

Strange—the biblical messages she'd been hearing and reading all her life, the ones she'd found tiresome a few weeks ago, came to her now so deep with meaning they might have been newly written just for her situation. That little spark of faith that had burned low in her these past few months while she struggled with one form of loss after another fed now and grew strong on the wisdom of God stored in her memory.

For several minutes Gypsy remained in her prayerful position, letting the healing words of the Lord wash, balmlike, through her sore thoughts. Then a sound, a slight squeak of the chapel door closing, told her someone else was in the room.

She sensed who it was even before she drew herself erect and turned to face Dayt standing beside her pew. Compassion flooded her heart at the sight of his features, haggard, unshaven, red-eyed with fatigue. His dirty work clothes made it plain he'd labored all night with a storm cleanup crew.

"G—good morning, Dayt," she stammered, suddenly struck reticent by guilt over the bitter denunciation she'd hurled at him the night of their quarrel. That and the sharp realization that for the rest of her days, she must *never* burden him with the knowledge that before he could call a halt to their once-blossoming relationship, she'd fallen irrevocably in love with him.

"Good morning, Gypsy," he returned, formal and constrained. "I . . . uh . . . know I must look like a bum . . . I wanted to check on Jody. And you."

"There's no reason to apologize," she assured him, matching his grave politeness. "I can see you've been clearing wreckage." There was a moment of awkward silence. "Here, sit down." She scooted over to make room for him beside her. What wouldn't she have given to put her arms around him, cradle his weary head and soothe away the harsh exhaustion lines etching his face? But, of course, that was out of the question.

"Yeah, that does sound good." He lowered himself slowly into the seat. "Just about a third of the Sauk Valley area is a mess. As you know." His words came brief and rough-edged with tiredness. "I'm . . . uh . . . I'm sorry, Gyps about your home. I didn't have a chance to tell you that yesterday, but I guess you know I'm sorry it had to go."

I will not cry. *I will not cry,* Gypsy forbade herself. "Yes." That's all she could push out over her distressed emotions.

"I stopped by Jode's room." Dayt turned to her; his eyes, hooded by a frown, pored over her as if he'd never really seen her before. "He told me you want him to live in Chicago with Ila. Is that so you can go back to Matt Morris . . . I mean . . . to work for him?"

It took all her effort to keep her eyes steady on his, so careful did Gypsy need to be to hide her love for this tough, uncompromising, thoroughly Christian man seated next to her, but she managed. "Do you mean, am I running out on my vow to raise Jody, even if I have to scrub floors to keep us together?"

He didn't answer. He continued to stare at her, his face drawn and unhappy, but for what reason she couldn't be sure.

"It's not a matter of what I *want*, Dayt. The important thing is, what's best for Jody?"

"I agree."

"Ila says he has real potential as an actor," she went on carefully, barely controlling the tremble in her lips. "And Ila . . . well . . . it's just as you've always said: she's a true woman of faith, so much better qualified than I am to guide Jody spiritually, and . . . and in *every* way. . . ." She broke off, head turned to hide her torment.

There was silence. Then she felt her rough, splintery hands lifted in Dayt's calloused ones.

"Is she?"

The tender, searching tone of Dayt's query drew Gypsy's eyes back to his. Her breath caught; in his gaze was the respect she'd long dreamed of seeing there!

He brought her bruised knuckles to his soft kiss, never letting go of her eyes. "Out in the Arizona desert, Gypsy, I had time to think, to step back and see you for what you really are."

"And—"

"I saw a young woman sacrificing her way of life for the boy who needed her. And then I came back and within one hour I found her tearing into that pile of rubble, laying down her life, literally, for him—"

Dayt's voice cracked; moisture filled his red-rimmed eyes. "Gypsy! Oh, Gypsy!" he said, his voice husky with emotion. "I had a lot of nerve to question your standing with the Lord. All the while I was *talking* about faith, you were *living* it. You humble me with your selflessness, Gypsy."

"Oh!" Gypsy's heart swelled; her captured right hand escaped to rise tentatively, then touch his rough cheek. "Don't say that, Dayt," she pleaded softly, tears dampening her own eyes. "You were my friend. There was a time— you could have talked me into just about anything, but you reached out to help instead."

"I wanted the best for you, Gypsy. Always, the best."

She shook her head wonderingly. "It's funny. Until the day of the storm, I didn't realize just how much faith I *did* have."

Dayt smiled and took her light-resting hand back into his warm clasp. "Sometimes belief sneaks up on us, honey."

He gestured toward the figure of Christ in the small window above the altar. "I spent years trying to keep Christ up in the stained glass windows. Didn't want him to come down and mix with my real life for fear I'd need to give up some . . . activities . . . I thought made me happy." He was looking beyond her, into a past she didn't share.

"But . . . they didn't satisfy you? The . . . activities?"

"No." With that quiet reply, he gently placed her hands in her lap and rose from the seat. He walked slowly to the altar table, his eyes fastened on its plain wooden cross. "No, Gypsy, as the years went by I got less and less satisfaction from the things I'd once thought more important than staying in touch with God. And then . . . ," He turned to her. "The ordeal of Ila and Tony Danova began. You know about that now, don't you?"

Gypsy, responding to the sorrow in his manner, sat forward, longing to share his concern. "Yes."

"I saw two wonderful people suffering. At first I was mad; why was God letting this happen?" He turned again toward the cross. "But it was through them I began to understand the power of Christ. Because they had him in their lives, Tony was able to meet his disease with a dignity, a concern for others that lifted him above pity. And Ila— she's made a life for herself that's worthwhile and contributive, even though her heart breaks a little each day."

Dayt took a step toward her. "Gypsy, it took me a long time to get all this straight, but now I know: Jesus' Spirit is at work in us, helping us be good . . . generous . . . loving. We can't push him away or evade him. He's to be welcomed as the greatest friend we'll ever have!"

The earnest glow in Dayt's face, the ring of conviction in his voice, pulled Gypsy to her feet.

"That's exactly the way I feel!"

Her fervent whisper was the last sound uttered for many seconds. In her heart the sweet pain of one-sided love mingled with joy that Dayt, like her, had found his place with the Lord.

Still she was finding it impossible to keep the state of her heart out of her eyes—they'd always given her away. She pivoted quickly toward the chapel door. "I promised Jody I'd be right back," she fibbed.

"Gypsy." The soft command stopped her, but she kept her back to Dayt. "About Jody—are you going to tell him the truth?"

"What?" She was startled into turning.

"Are you going to tell him what he means to you?"

"I . . . don't want to burden him with guilt if he wants to go with Ila." She couldn't look at him; tears burned her violet eyes.

Strong, warm hands took her shoulders; one of them carefully forced her averted face toward his. "Gypsy, you're too young to be his mother, but it doesn't make any difference, does it? He's like your flesh and blood, all the same."

She nodded yes, mute with anguish.

"The boy loves you; and he needs you—both of us—a lot worse than he needs an acting career right now. If he's got talent, it'll still be there when he's grown up."

"But . . . I promised him he could choose."

"So we'll let him, but I know who he'll choose. How could he—how could *anyone* lucky enough to have your love turn away from it?"

The whole world stood still for Gypsy. Forever after,

she'd remember as the happiest moment of her life the instant when she looked up to see the unmistakable love in Dayt's eyes.

"Dayt, are you saying . . . ?" she managed to say over the surge in her heart.

"I'm saying I love you, Mary Catherine Connor; I love you every way a man could love a woman. If you'll have me," he whispered huskily, "I want to marry you just as fast as the law allows!"

"Oh . . . *Dayt!*" She was in his arms, crushed as they clung to each other like two shipwreck survivors. The strong, clean current of their love flowed from one to the other through arms aching with tenderness.

"Dayt! Oh, my love! Can you forgive me for the awful accusations I made against you that night?"

"Gypsy, honey, I was an arrogant fool to discuss expansion plans with Ila before I'd talked them over with you," he muttered into her hair, "but the truth is, I was already counting my chickens. Every time I looked at you this summer, I was seeing you presiding over our home at O'Rourke Farms by next year. I assumed you'd be willing to give up the boardinghouse for that. I . . . guess that was pretty egotistical of me?"

Gypsy laughed, her heart soaring in happy flight. "Uh-huh. But like Gramps once told me, two egos the size of ours are bound to create a lot of electricity! A heartstorm!"

Dayt joined her laughter. Then he tipped her head back to kiss her with gently possessive lips.

"Now," he said tenderly, "let's go talk to Jody. Whether or not he decides to go with Ila, I want him to be our boy. Our legally adopted son."

chapter

12

MOONLIGHT, THE DEEP HARVEST-GOLD of a late October midnight moon, stole in through the big-paned floor-to-ceiling window opposite the huge bed. It flowed over the simple elegance of the white taffeta wedding dress draped carefully over an armchair, caught in the feathery-fine lace of the antique veil worn by four generations of O'Rourke brides and now trailing off the corner of a dresser, glistened on the pale peach satin and lace negligee of the figure standing rapt by the window frame gazing out into the light and shadow of a sweeping, oak-punctuated lawn.

Gypsy shivered, not with cold, but with a delicious, shimmery memory of a wedding night so tender, so beautiful, so sacred she wasn't sure it was reality.

A rustle of the sheets and comforter, and a man's rumbly words, "Gypsy? Baby?" turned her toward the bed where Dayt pushed himself up against the headboard. "Honey, what's the matter?" he exclaimed, pulling on his robe as he got out of bed to come to her side.

"Oh, Dayt, not a thing!" she assured him. "Only—just look." She pointed as he came up behind her and slipped his arms protectively around her. "Over there, where the timber starts, see? Two deer. Aren't they *beautiful?*" She sighed, pulling his arms tight and snuggling into his embrace.

"Mmmm," he agreed into the fluff of her soft, scented curls. "But why are you out of bed, sweetheart?"

She turned in his arms, leaning into the sinewy strength of her husband of a few hours. Then she took his clean-angled face in soft hands. "Is it real?" she whispered wonderingly. "Are we really married? Or am I dreaming again that you and I have been together—will be to-gether—forever?"

The answer was a long, searching kiss that pulled her off the floor, stretching her on ecstatic tiptoes.

"Are you as happy as I am, Baby-kitten?" Dayt murmured when they stopped for breath.

"Oh, yes!"

"Sure you don't mind our spending our first night at O'Rourke Farms?"

"Oh, honey! There's *nowhere* else I'd rather have spent my wedding night!"

He chuckled, running a hardened fingertip over her eyelids, down her nose to her lips. "Well, I certainly had no intention of passing our first night on a plane to Hawaii! We'll leave tomorrow at a nice, sensible ten o'clock in the morning, and check into the Royal Hawaiian bridal suite just in time for a late dinner tomorrow night. Moonlight dining on our own balcony overlooking Waikiki Beach."

"Umm!" She laughed and cuddled into his chest. "The perfect honeymoon for the perfect wedding. Wasn't it lovely—the wedding, I mean? And the reception: how many couples can say they had their wedding reception in a barn?"

"I loved it. Made me feel like your grandpa was there with us."

"He was, Dayt. I know he was," she answered softly. "And your folks—they were so nice about staying at the motel instead of out here."

"I should think so!"

"And Aunt May and Uncle Worth just insisted Jody stay on with them till we get back from Hawaii."

"I should think so!"

"Wasn't Jody the sweetest best man ever? Oh, Dayt, I'm so glad he wants to be our boy!" Then a sobering thought struck her. "There was only one part of the day that made me sad, Dayt. That was when Ila sang, and I thought how hard it must be for her to see us so happy, when . . . when—"

Dayt lifted her face to his. "Gypsy, darling, no one knows where his life may lead. But we've put our trust in Jesus, just as Ila and Tony did. If it were the other way around, would you begrudge Ila all the happiness she could have?"

"No, of course not," Gypsy answered sincerely. "That's why I deeded Jesse's Barn over to her, Dayt. I have so much; if the theater will bring a little bit of fulfillment into her life—" Gypsy stopped, unable to go on.

"It will, honey. And your decision to study music with her—as far as I'm concerned, you don't have to do one thing more to be the best natural musician I know, but it'll give her so much pleasure to—"

Smiling, Gypsy finished his sentence, "To teach me a whole bunch of stuff I should have learned years ago! I'm looking forward to it."

213

"And I'm looking forward to hearing the fruits of your learning!" Dayt laughed. Then his eyes grew distant as he remembered something else. "Ila told old me after the ceremony that in her heart, she and Tony are still the same man and wife they became eight years ago, united forever in God's love." Dayt looked at Gypsy, his gaze steady, as if he were repeating again the marriage vows. "That's the way it will always be for us."

"God bless her!" Gypsy's wish was a prayer straight from her heart. "And us."

"Amen. And now, Mrs. O'Rourke," Dayt said, picking her up in arms made just for carrying her, "I think it's time for us to go back to bed."

"Dayt," she whispered, face buried in his strong neck, "I think I'd better tell you what I was praying for last night."

"Ummm? What outrageous thing did you think up?" he teased, bearing her effortlessly toward the bed.

She planted a feather-soft kiss on the corner of his mouth. "That Jody won't be an only child!"

He laughed; she laughed; their voices twined in joyous agreement.

"Gypsy, my wonderful, storm-hearted, lovable wife," Dayt murmured, setting her on her feet, "that's one prayer I'll do my best to help God answer!"

ABOUT THE AUTHOR

CAROL BLAKE GERROND has taught high school English and speech for a quarter century. During that time, she directed some sixty plays, many of which she wrote. "I specialize in serious messages wrapped in robust American humor," she says.

Carol has published six short romances in a national magazine. This is her first inspirational romance for Serenade Books.

The mother of three grown children, Carol lives in Illinois with her husband of thirty-two years and a Himalayan cat. She's played the organ in her church since she was a freshman in high school.

A Letter to Our Readers

Dear Reader:

Welcome to Serenade Books—a series designed to bring you beautiful love stories in the world of inspirational romance. They will uplift you, encourage you, and provide hours of wholesome entertainment, so thousands of readers have testified. That we might better contribute to your reading enjoyment, we would appreciate your taking a few minutes to respond to the following questions and return to:

> Lois Taylor
> Serenade Books
> The Zondervan Publishing House
> 1415 Lake Drive, S.E.
> Grand Rapids, Michigan   49506

1. Did you enjoy reading *Heartstorm?*

   ☐ Very much. I would like to see more books by this author!
   ☐ Moderately
   ☐ I would have enjoyed it more if _____

2. Where did you purchase this book? _____

3. What influenced your decision to purchase this book?

   ☐ Cover   ☐ Back cover copy
   ☐ Title   ☐ Friends
   ☐ Publicity   ☐ Other _____

4. Please rate the following elements from 1 (poor) to 10 (superior).

☐ Heroine   ☐ Plot
☐ Hero   ☐ Inspirational theme
☐ Setting   ☐ Secondary characters

5. What are some inspirational themes you would like to see treated in future books?

_____

_____

6. Please indicate your age range:

☐ Under 18   ☐ 25–34   ☐ 46–55
☐ 18–24   ☐ 35–45   ☐ Over 55

Serenade / Saga books are inspirational romances in historical settings, designed to bring you a joyful, heart-lifting reading experience.

Serenade / Saga books available in your local bookstore:

Serenade/Saga books are now being published in a new, longer length:

Serenade / Serenata books are inspirational romances in contemporary settings, designed to bring you a joyful, heart-lifting reading experience.

Serenade / Serenata books available in your local bookstore:

Serenade/Serenata books are now being published in a new, longer length:

Watch for other books in both the *Serenade/Saga* (historical) and *Serenade/Serenata* (contemporary) series, coming soon.